UNDER THE HARVEST MOON
Book 7 Jacob's Daughter series

WRITTEN BY
Samantha Jillian Bayarr

All scripture references in this book used from New International Version of the Bible

www.LivingstonHallPublishers.blogspot.com

If you enjoy discussing Amish Fiction with other readers, join my Facebook Group, Amish Friendship Bread

Includes a BONUS RECIPE by Diana Montgomery for…
DUTCH COUNTRY PUMPKIN ROLLS

Also by Samantha Jillian Bayarr

Jacob's Daughter Amish Series
Jacob's Daughter
Amish Winter Wonderland
Under the Mulberry Tree
Amish Winter of Promises
Chasing Fireflies
Amish Summer of Courage
Under the Harvest Moon

Amish Winter Collection
An Amish Christmas Wish
Amish White Christmas
Amish Love Letters

LWF Amish Series
Little Wild Flower Book I
Little Wild Flower Book II
The Taming of a Wild Flower
Little Wild Flower in Bloom
Little Wild Flower's Journey

Amish Romance
The Quilter's Son
The Amish Gardener

Christian Romance
Milk Maid in Heaven
The Anniversary
A Sheriff's Legacy: Book One (Historical)
Preacher Outlaw: Book Two (Historical)

Amish Love Series
An Amish Harvest
An Amish Courtship
An Amish Widower
Amish Sisters
Please check online for availability.

CHAPTER 1

"Come quick!" Rachel pleaded with Doctor Davis from the phone at her *Aenti* Bess's B&B. "*Mei aenti's* rolling on the floor holding her stomach. Something's really wrong with her! I can't get her to stop crying long enough to ask her what happened!"

Rachel wasn't sure what the doctor could do for her *Aenti,* but Bess had given her a strict warning not to call for an ambulance—even if her appendix burst. She wouldn't tell the woman that the doc insisted on sending an ambulance anyway.

For a moment, Rachel considered whether she should leave Bess to look for her husband, Jessup, but his horse and buggy wasn't in the barn when she'd arrived, and Bess's screams had prompted her into the *haus*. Taking a deep breath, Rachel ran back to tend to her crying *aenti*, whose screams became louder the closer she came to the kitchen entrance. Right where she'd left her, Bess lay sprawled across the floor in a puddle of water. Her deep blue dress was soaked and clung to her skin as the poor woman doubled over, groaning from the pain.

Rachel scanned the kitchen for a possible source of the water, but realized the puddle was only under Bess. It hadn't been there when she'd gone into the parlor to call for the doctor.

She'd seen this before!

"*Aenti,* can you get up so I can move you to the sofa? I think you might be more comfortable there until the doctor gets here."

"*Nee,*" she groaned before doubling at her ample waistline.

Bess had always been a thick woman, and Rachel knew there was no way she could get her to the sofa without some cooperation from the woman.

Rachel gulped. "*Aenti,* I don't mean to pry, but when was your last cycle?"

Bess suddenly opened her eyes and glared at her niece. "I went through the change about the same time I married Jessup," she grunted. "*Ach,* am I hemorrhaging? It feels like my insides are trying to come outside of me." She reached down and felt the dampness of her dress, and then brought her hand to her face for examination. Confused at the lack of what she thought would be blood on her dampened hand, Bess looked to Rachel quizzically.

"You're not bleeding, but I suspect you might be—having a *boppli!*

"Nee, that's impossible," she grunted and bore down. "I'm old and already went through the change. Doctor Davis even said it was so."

It wasn't impossible. Bess was only in her early fifties. Many of the women in the community had *bopplies* well into their fifties.

Bess grunted again and cried out. "I have to go to the washroom."

Rachel had no idea how she would get her there, but she suspected Bess was feeling a need to bear down. Bess and Jessup had been married for more than a year now, and the woman had always been so plump that she could easily disguise a pregnancy in the folds of her girth. But how could she have gone this long without knowing she was pregnant? Was it even possible? Rachel supposed at her age, Bess and Doctor Davis both would have assumed the change before a pregnancy. Since her *Aenti* had never been pregnant before, she wouldn't have known to look for it. But how was it that none of her *familye* had even suspected?

"Can you get up?" Rachel asked in-between the woman's cries.

Bess shook her head frantically as she held her breath and grunted. "I'm sorry for the mess I'm about to make. I can't make this urge stop."

Suddenly Bess's face turned pale. "I think my womb just fell out. Maybe—you should call for that ambulance." She began to cry and Rachel soothed her.

Rachel approached her next statement with care, hoping she wouldn't offend her *aenti.* "I should make certain you are not bleeding."

"Hurry," Bess cried. "If I'm dying and you can save me, then do what you have to."

Rachel could hear the sudden panic in Bess's voice, and wondered if she should reassure her by admitting that an ambulance was on its way. Reluctantly, Rachel lifted the water-soaked dress to see what was happening. Both joy and anxiety filled her as she spotted the crown of a *boppli's* head.

Rachel looked at Bess sternly. "I need you to push as hard as you can when the pain seizes you again. I can see the *boppli's* head."

There was no time for either of them to think about it. Within seconds Bess grunted and pushed with a loud screech. Rachel eased out one shoulder, cradling the head just before the wee one slipped from her *aenti's* womb. Tears filled Rachel's eyes, emotion constricting her throat as Bess rested her head on the linoleum from pure exhaustion, the pains finally subsiding.

Rachel used the corner of her apron to wipe the *boppli's* mouth, causing him to let out a wail. Bess's head popped up from the floor and stared at the wiggling infant in Rachel's hands.

Immediately, Rachel handed him to his *mamm* as she watched her *aenti's* expression turn from shock to sheer joy as she reached for her *boppli.* Bess cradled the infant in her arms while Rachel pulled a pillow and lap quilt from the sofa to make her *aenti* more comfortable until help arrived. After tucking the pillow under her head, she reached up onto the table and grabbed yarn and a pair of sheers where Bess had been crocheting before the pains had consumed her. Rachel tied the length of yarn in two spots onto the cord and snipped it with the sewing sheers.

Bess hadn't taken her eyes off her new son and hadn't paid any attention to Rachel's bustling about her kitchen. By the dreamy look in her *aenti's* eyes, Rachel could tell she was enamored with her unexpected gift.

CHAPTER 2

Jessup burst in the back door of the B&B, shock paling his face. He looked at his *fraa* lying on the kitchen floor, a *boppli* in her arms, while Rachel sopped up water from the floor around her.

Rachel looked up from the chore. "*Onkel* Jessup, I think *aenti* has something to tell you."

Bess looked up from the wiggling bundle in her arms long enough to beckon her husband to her side. "*Kume,* meet your new son."

Jessup nearly fell over. He stepped back and caught himself against a kitchen chair as he stared at his *fraa.* His heart raced, but strangely, no pain existed there. He put his hand to his chest. Was he having a heart attack, but was in too much shock to notice the pain?

Jessup looked at the *boppli* in Bess's arms, and at the expression on her face. He'd seen that look before from his deceased *fraa* when she'd borne him his *kinner*. Now he was a new *daed* again. Was he ready for this? Would his aging body hold out long enough to watch the wee one grow to be a *mann?*

A thrilling fear gripped Jessup, but he swallowed it as he knelt close to his *fraa's* head to place a kiss on her forehead. He placed a hand over the *boppli's* head and smoothed his dark hair. Tears welled up in his eyes as he felt pure love for his *fraa* and new son.

"He's really ours?" Jessup asked with a shaky voice.

"He is a miracle, *jah?"* Bess asked.

"I suppose the doc was wrong about you going through the change," Jessup chuckled.

They both laughed and cried at the same time, as Jessup cradled his *familye* in his arms. To start over with his *fraa* was truly a miracle, *jah.*

Rachel entered the room, holding another quilt she'd taken from the spare room upstairs, and handed it to her *onkel.*

"If we wrap the *boppli,* then we can get *Aenti* into her own bed where she might be more comfortable while we wait for Doctor Davis."

As Rachel wrapped the *boppli* in the quilt, Doctor Davis walked in through the kitchen. With the door open, they could hear the siren from the ambulance nearing the B&B.

Doctor Davis looked to each of the faces, and then focused on the bundle in Rachel's arms. "What happened here? Bess, are you alright?"

Bess let out an unusual giggle none of them had ever heard before. "I had a *boppli!* I wasn't going through the change after all. I was pregnant!"

Doctor Davis smiled. "It's not the first time I've been wrong."

Jessup shook the doctor's hand. "I'm mighty glad you were wrong *this* time. He's a handsome fella, ain't so?"

They shook hands vigorously. "Yes, he is. Let's get momma into her own bed if we can, so I can examine her. How are you feeling, Bess?"

"I couldn't be better. Did you call for an ambulance?"

Doctor Davis nodded. "I was worried it was something serious, so I called for one as a precaution. Do you want them to stand by until I make sure everything is alright?"

Bess shook her head as she admired her newborn son. "Everything is fine. Send them away."

Rachel followed the two *menner* into the bedroom, her new little cousin resting peacefully in her arms. It seemed strange and natural at the same time for Rachel to recognize who the *boppli* was in connection to her.

Once Bess was safely in her own room, she asked Rachel to help her into her nightgown. Rachel handed the *boppli* to Doctor Davis, and then went to the bureau to get fresh linen bedclothes for her *aenti*. Doctor Davis busied himself examining the new arrival while Rachel fussed with Bess to get her settled. Jessup quickly left the room to meet the ambulance and to send them on their way.

Doctor Davis pulled the stethoscope from his ears. "That's one strong boy you have there."

Rachel excused herself to make some tea for her *aenti*. When she entered the kitchen, she realized she'd almost forgotten about the mess on the floor. *Aenti* would be in no condition to take on her house chores for at least a week, depending on what the doc said to her. But given her age, Rachel imagined her *aenti* would be bound to bed-rest for at least that long.

Inside the mudroom, Rachel found a bucket, a stack of clean rags, and a scrub brush she knew she could use to clean the floor. She filled the bucket and set to work after putting on the kettle for tea.

Blake entered the kitchen while Rachel was finishing up the floor. He looked at her a little strangely.

"Why is the doc's buggy here?"

Rachel emptied the bucket of dirty water out the back door and wrung out the rags she'd used beneath her feet to "mop" the floor. "Doctor Davis is here for *Aenti*."

Blake looked around at the disheveled kitchen.

"What happened here?"

The tea kettle whistled and Rachel wiped her hands on her apron so she could remove it before it lost all its water through the steam cap. Rachel looked back at Blake, her eyes gleaming. "*Aenti* Bess had a *boppli.*"

Blake chuckled. "A baby? I didn't know she was expecting."

Rachel laughed. "Neither did poor *Aenti*. She had an awful time of it. No one was here, so I had to deliver him."

"Him? She has a boy? Jessup has to be beside himself."

"*Mei onkel* is quite beside himself indeed." Rachel laughed at the sound of her own statement. "I can't believe those two didn't know she was expecting. *Aenti* assumed it was the change she was going through, but this is such a *wunderbaar* blessing."

Blake pulled Rachel into his arms and nuzzled her neck. "By this time next year, we could have a *boppli* of our own."

Rachel felt heat rise in her cheeks at the thought of having Blake's *kinner.* "Maybe we should concentrate on getting married first. I can't believe we are to be married in less than two weeks! This past year has gone by so fast."

Blake pulled away from her and drew a letter from his pocket. "I finally got a letter from Bruce."

Rachel's ears perked up at the sound of her kidnapper's name. It was hard for Rachel to believe that it had been more than a year since her ordeal with Blake's father, but she felt safe knowing he'd been in prison the entire time.

"By the look on your face, it must be *gut* news," Rachel said, trying not to worry.

CHAPTER 3

Blake held the letter up in front of his face, a faint smile forming on his lips. "I'm guessing that having a year to sober up and reflect on his lifetime of mistakes has been good for him. His letter says he started attending the church services they have at the chapel in the prison."

"That is *gut* news. I suspect you still have cause for concern. You look a little stressed."

Blake pulled the straw hat from his head and placed it on a hook near the kitchen door. Looping his fingers in his suspenders, he let them snap against his muscular chest. "He doesn't understand why I took the baptism to become Amish. He thinks I did it just for you. I've tried explaining to him that because of my baptism I was able to forgive him for kidnapping you and shooting me. I'm hoping that the church-going will open his eyes. It's obviously bringing him around a little bit or he wouldn't have written back to me after all this time."

"We can continue to keep him in our prayers," Rachel offered. "Surely *Gott* will soften his heart."

Blake let out a breath in a whoosh. "I pray that it is so. But his letter didn't sound as remorseful as I'd hoped."

Rachel wrapped her arms around Blake and placed a soft kiss on his neck. "You've done your part by forgiving him. The rest is up to him. Perhaps in time."

❧ ❧ ❧

Jessup couldn't take his eyes off his new son. He cradled the wee one in his arms while Doctor Davis finished his examination of Bess. He couldn't wait to show him off to his older *kinner* and the rest of his *familye.*

For now, he would savor this moment and cherish it, remembering how quickly *bopplies* grow. His immediate thought was to get the cradle he'd made for his first-born, but it had been left behind in Nappanee along with most of their belongings when they'd moved to the B&B. Their *mudder* could never part with the cradle or quilts and such, saying they could someday be used for *grandkinner.* But after her death, Jessup couldn't bear to see them. As far as he knew, the items had remained undisturbed in the attic of his farm *haus* that his eldest *bruder* had moved into after Jessup had left Nappanee. Surely Bess would want to make new things for the *boppli* in the meantime, but he aimed to get that cradle somehow.

When the doctor finished with Bess, Jessup pulled the ladder-back chair next to the bed, his new son tucked in his other arm. He looked up into his *fraa's* dreamy face and smiled.

"What shall we call him?"

Bess managed a weak smile. "I was thinking since he is my first, and probably my last *boppli*, that I should give him the name Adam."

Jessup smiled. "*Das gut.* It's a strong name for such a strong *buwe.*"

Jessup couldn't help but feel a swell of pride as he gazed lovingly upon his *boppli.* The wee one represented a new start for him. He'd been feeling his age recently as his *kinner* continued to grow older. His oldest would be out on his own in just a few short years, but with a new *bruder* in the *haus,* perhaps the *buwe* wouldn't seem so eager to grow up.

Bess closed her eyes, feeling too sleepy to resist a little nap. With Jessup and her new *boppli* securely next to her, she yielded to her body's prompting to let sleep overtake her. Jessup slipped out of the room with Adam in his arms. Once he was in the kitchen, he handed the *boppli* over to Rachel.

"I need to call Hiram to give him the news of his *schweschder's boppli.* Won't he be surprised? I suppose I will make calls to the rest of our *familye*. If Bess wakes up, let her know where I am."

Blake winked at Rachel as he followed Jessup into the front parlor of the B&B. She knew they would most likely be preoccupied for a while, so she took the *boppli* into the private sitting room to relax in the rocking chair. It had been a long day, and she hadn't made it back to bakery to reopen for the afternoon.

"I don't care if my customers missed me this afternoon," she cooed at little Adam. "I wouldn't have passed up the opportunity to help bring you into this world for all the customers in Elkhart County."

If Rachel hadn't come over early to have lunch with *Aenti* Bess, the woman would have been on her own. The thought made Rachel shudder. The thing she was most grateful for was that there were presently no guests staying at the B&B. One thing was certain, though, they would either have to close down temporarily, or hire someone to run the place until *Aenti* Bess was back on her feet.

She peered down at little Adam sleeping trustfully in her arms.

Danki, Gott for this little miracle.

CHAPTER 4

Lila King looked out across the room of the crowded bus station. Most everyone was being greeted or sent off by a loved-one, but not her. She was waiting for a stranger to pick her up. She felt foreign among a sea of *Englischers* as she leaned against *Onkel* Jessup's handmade cradle. It was large and heavy, and she'd had to have assistance from the driver to haul the cradle into the waiting area of the bus station.

The musty air of the station was stifling and almost nauseating when coupled with the smell of diesel fuel exhaust that drifted in through the open doors from where the busses sat in the holding area just outside with their motors running.

Lila's attention suddenly wavered to the doorway where a handsome Amish *mann* entered. It was as if she had somehow sensed his presence. She could see the blue in his eyes from where she sat, and the dimples that formed at his instant smile when his gaze met hers were enough to unseat her. She wondered—no hoped—it wasn't Samuel Yoder, *Onkel* Jessup's new nephew to come for her. Her *onkel* had sent for her after the news of a *boppli* that had shocked the entire *familye*. With no other relatives to take care of the B&B, while the new parents tended to their unexpected blessing, Lila was the logical choice to provide her services to the *familye*. Besides, it had been urgent for her to get the handmade cradle to her *onkel* to use for his new *boppli.* Now, Lila was certain she would have to endure the discomfort of riding with this handsome stranger.

The young *mann* approached her with the sort of confidence Lila would deem to be somewhat prideful, but still charming. "Are you Lila?" he asked.

"*Jah.* You must be Samuel." Her voice shook nervously.

Samuel bent down to pick up her bag and the wooden cradle, and then he walked toward the door without another word to her. Would the ride to her *onkel's haus* be filled with the same reserve? She was fairly certain she didn't want to engage in conversation with Samuel, but neither was she fond of awkward silence. She forced herself to believe that awkward silence was better than letting this *mann's* alluring smile distract her from the pact she'd made with herself to not become caught up with marriage and having *kinner* the way her friends had. Since her *mamm* had died minutes after giving birth to her, she had determined, even at a young age that she would not risk bringing *kinner* into the world only to leave them without a *mamm* the way she'd grown up.

Lila sighed, knowing that the ride in close-quarters with such a handsome *mann* would not be an easy test of her willpower. But she'd been able to resist the advances of every suitor for the past few years who had come to ask her to take buggy rides with them. She could handle a short buggy ride with Samuel, especially since she would most likely not see him again.

Lila tried not to show her discomfort as Samuel's leg rested so close to hers she could feel his body heat. Never mind that it was a chilly day, and there didn't seem to be a lap-quilt in the buggy.

Samuel slapped the reins against the gelding's muscular flank. "I hope the weather stays cool without freezing for the next couple of weeks so it will be nice for the wedding."

Be polite, but not encouraging. He doesn't have to know I would rather not talk to him.

"*Mei schweschder,* Rachel, is marrying Blake Monroe," he continued. "There is much to be done to prepare. It's *gut* timing for your visit so you can help with preparations at the B&B since that is where the wedding is to take place. The *familye* was concerned that with the arrival of the new *boppli,* that it would slow the progress, but you will be a *gut* addition. I'm certain Rachel will be grateful for the extra help."

Wunderbaar, Lila groaned inwardly. *I didn't realize that Onkel was volunteering me to help with a wedding!*

Lila didn't allow herself to swoon over *bopplies* or weddings the way her friends and cousins did. She was against all of it, and would just as soon steer clear of any part of it. Unfortunately, her *daed* had put her into a tight spot, where both situations would be clearly unavoidable.

"I imagine you're eager to see the new *boppli. Mei schweschders* and *mamm* have already spoiled him. Most women are *narrish* when they learn of a new *boppli,* and they all have to visit and make clothes and quilts."

She wasn't crazy over the presence of a new *boppli,* but she would not admit that to this handsome stranger.

She smiled politely. *"Onkel* Jessup said I was to take over the duties at the B&B to keep it running."

"Jah, but there are no reservations set until Christmas, so he will most likely ask you to help with wedding preparations or to help *Aenti* Bess with the *boppli.*

Lila had no intention of helping with the *boppli,* but the only alternative was to assist with preparing for something she did not believe in—a wedding. How could she help with something she was so much against? It would be the first time she would meet her new cousins, and she was not getting off to a very *gut* start.

Samuel flashed her a sideways glance while keeping his eye on the busy road ahead. "You *do* like weddings, don't you?"

CHAPTER 5

When Samuel steered the gelding into the circle drive of the B&B, Lila could not get out of the buggy fast enough. Most girls would daydream about having Samuel pull them into an embrace, and wrapping his work-strong arms around them.

Not her.

She had spent nearly the entire buggy ride pushing such thoughts from her mind to avoid giving into something that could never be a part of her life. In her mind, it was best to be casual and cordial, but nothing more.

Lila didn't wait for Samuel to fetch her bag from the back of the buggy. While he tied his horse, she was nearly up the steps to the B&B with it, and didn't dare look back. It wasn't her intention to be rude, but when he brought in the cradle, she would thank him for the ride to her *aenti's haus* in the presence of *familye*. This way she could avoid any lingering conversation with him. The buggy ride had seemed excruciatingly lengthy because of the long silence between them, but she'd made it very clear to Samuel that she was not interested in being overly friendly. It was better that way. It was best not to give him any reason to ask to call on her company.

Samuel took his time with his horse, making certain there was fresh water in the trough. He patted the side of his gelding's nose. "Do you think that girl is a mite shy, or do you think she has a beau?"

The gelding nickered and bobbed his head.

"You're right. A girl that handsome probably has the *menner* lining up to visit with her at Sunday Singings."

Samuel moved to the open door of the buggy and retrieved the handmade cradle. He knew Jessup had been eager for it to arrive. And not a day too soon since that *boppli* was already three days old. He'd overheard his *mamm* and *schweschders* talking about Jessup's unhappiness over having to place his new son in a wicker laundry basket packed with a quilt. Samuel didn't see what the big deal was. In fact, he'd thought it was a pretty *gut* idea. But what did he know? He wasn't married with *kinner* of his own. Even though his twin *schweschder* was about to get married, Samuel didn't have a sweetheart or even any prospects.

It wasn't until he met Lila just now that he'd even given it any thought before. What was it about her that prompted such thoughts in him? Perhaps it was her aloof behavior. He was used to the girls in the community paying a lot of attention to him, but he hadn't found one yet that he had any real interest in—until now. He could have his pick of any girl in the community, so why did he suddenly find himself wanting this one?

Samuel let himself in through the kitchen door of the B&B. He could smell the woodsy smell of the fireplace even before he heard the crackling and popping. It brought warmth to his bones from the chill of the late afternoon. Jessup greeted him before he made it to the small sitting room on the private side of the B&B.

Jessup's face lit up at the sight of the cradle tucked under Samuel's arm.

"When Lila didn't come in with it, I worried for a minute."

Jessup took the cradle and gazed upon it as though it was made from pure gold. "I never thought I would have to use this again unless it was for *grandkinner*. Isn't it funny how life changes sometimes? Just when you don't expect *Gott* could give you anymore, he blesses you one more time."

Tears welled up in his eyes as he walked to the back stairwell that led to the private living quarters.

Not knowing what to do with himself, Samuel walked back to the kitchen to make a pot of fresh *kaffi* to keep him warm on his trip home. The sun had begun to sink below the tree-line, and it was starting to feel like the end of October out there. The first week of November would be a little colder, but Samuel prayed the weather would hold steady until his *schweschder's* wedding.

Lila entered the room and turned to leave when she saw Samuel. He looked up at her and beckoned her back into the room.

"You want some *kaffi?* The ride here was a little chilly. I'm sorry I forgot to put the lap quilts back in the buggy."

Lila nodded shyly and eyed the cupboards wondering which one contained the cups.

Samuel could see what she was asking without saying a word. He pointed to the cupboard to her right. "The cups are in that one."

He pulled on the utensil drawer. "Spoons are in here." Then pointed to the narrow cupboard beside her. "Sugar and honey are in there."

"Danki," she said almost too quiet for him to hear.

Samuel was used to the women in his life being outspoken. He had his work cut out for him if he was ever going to get this one to feel comfortable enough around him to talk. From the few words she'd spoken, he knew she had a lovely voice. It was gentle and angelic—one he could get used to listening to for the rest of his life.

Lila cleared her throat. "The *kaffi* is ready."

Samuel's face heated. Had she noticed him daydreaming? "*Danki*," he muttered as he poured *kaffi* into the cups Lila had set beside him.

He looked into her angelic face as she sipped the hot beverage cautiously. He wanted to ask her to the Sunday Singing tomorrow evening, but he suddenly lost his nerve. What was wrong with him? He'd always been at ease when talking to women. Was his sudden inability to form more than two words because she appeared to not be interested in him?

CHAPTER 6

Lila scooped the pumpkin seeds and fleshy insides from the freshly-picked gourd. Now that she'd been at her *onkel's haus* for three days, she'd settled into a routine. Her duties were a lot different than what she'd been expecting when she was asked to help, but she didn't mind. As long as she wasn't being asked to tend to the *boppli,* Lila would be content with taking over the kitchen duties and assisting with wedding preparations for Rachel.

Mashing the pumpkin in the mixing bowl, she hoped her loaves of bread would be enough for the *familye* dinner that Jessup had asked her to cook for. Lila intended to serve the dinner in the large dining area that was normally for guests, hoping the distance would keep her from contact with Samuel. She knew he would be attending, but what she didn't know was why it worried her the way it did.

She refused to admit to herself that she could be attracted to his baritone voice or his lively blue eyes that seemed to dance with constant delight.

Lila mindlessly knocked the bowl with the pumpkin seeds onto the floor.

Oh no, they're ruined. Now I can't roast them! I better stop daydreaming and concentrate on what I'm doing so I don't shame onkel with my carelessness.

Bending down to clean the mess, she wondered if she would always be happy working in someone else's kitchen. It hadn't struck her until just now that she could be tending her *mamm's* kitchen in the deceased woman's absence for the rest of her life—as a spinster.

"Do you need some help?"

The strong baritone voice startled her, causing her to bump her head on the underside of the table. Lila rested on her haunches, rubbing the sore spot on the top of her head as she glared at Samuel.

He reached a hand to assist her, but she refused, scooping up the last of the spilled pumpkin and placing it back in its bowl.

"I didn't mean to startle you. Sounds like you hit your head pretty hard. I think it's bleeding on the top." He reached out toward the back of her head, but she flinched away from him.

"At least sit down for a minute and let me get you a wet towel so we can make sure you don't need the doc to come and stitch you up."

She reluctantly obeyed his gentle urging, but only because her scalp stung and her head wouldn't stop pounding. She reached up and touched the tender spot, and then instinctively drew her hand in front of her face. She dizzied at the sight of blood on her fingers.

Samuel rushed to her side with a wet dishrag, pressing it to the wound. "Hold this for a minute. Put pressure on it. Head wounds always bleed a lot."

She replaced her hand on the dishrag, wincing at the pressure she placed on the injury. Samuel unpinned her *kapp,* causing her to gasp. She automatically reached up with her other hand and tried to stop him.

Samuel gazed into her eyes, momentarily hypnotizing her with the blue depths that pleaded with her to trust him.

Lila allowed him to unpin her hair to better reach the abrasion on her scalp that suddenly didn't hurt anymore.

Samuel ran his fingers through the tresses of Lila's sun-streaked chestnut hair, trying desperately to focus on assessing the severity of the laceration. He had never had his fingers in a woman's hair before, and the sensation drew him to her in a loving way.

Lila couldn't help but be mesmerized by the feel of Samuel's fingers trolling across her scalp. Until now, she had remained untouched by any *mann.* How would she ever be able to resist such an awareness of his touch for the remainder of her stay here? Out of necessity, she steeled her emotions against him, suddenly becoming rigid.

Lila jumped from her chair suddenly. "Does it need stitches?"

Samuel, caught off guard by her sudden change of demeanor, shook his head. *"Nee."*

Lila narrowed her mouth. "Then please leave me alone to finish making the meal. It's getting late, and I don't have time to worry about a little scrape on my head when I have to prepare a meal for the entire *familye."*

Until she suddenly changed her tone to reflect harshness, Samuel had been tempted to meet Lila's full lips with his. He conceded, knowing his *schweschders* would arrive any moment to assist her with the meal. He looked into her steely hazel eyes once more before exiting the room. He'd seen vulnerability in those eyes just moments before, and he couldn't bear to gaze upon the indifference he saw there now. What had imprinted such hardness of her heart that it should reflect in her eyes?

Samuel left the room, his exposed heart feeling the twinge of pain from her steely gaze. Had it been his imagination that he'd felt her respond to him? He was certain he hadn't mistaken the dreamy look in her eyes at his touch that was quickly replaced with such melancholy he could hardly bear it. Why did he feel such a strong desire to be the one to break through the sadness in her heart? He barely knew her, but yet he wanted to be the one to shelter her and bring joy to her heart.

賈

Lila chided herself for letting her guard down long enough to let Samuel affect her the way he had, as she twisted her hair back into a tight bun at the back of her head. She had no desire to become romantically involved with any *mann*. Her lifelong stance had been never to wed and never to bring a *boppli* into the world full of the sort of emptiness she had endured from growing up without a *mamm*. No relative had been able to fill the gap that her *mamm* had left in her heart when she'd died moments after giving birth to her. She would not risk doing the same thing to a *boppli* of her own.

CHAPTER 7

Samuel couldn't help but stare at Lila as she placed the plate in front of him. She had not made eye-contact with him at all as she moved about the room making certain everything was in place. Her reluctance to sit with the *familye* during the meal did not go unnoticed. She seemed friendly enough with his *schweschders,* causing him to wonder if it was not the world she loathed, but him. But when Rachel tried to pass little Adam to Lila, Samuel saw Lila's reaction and couldn't help but wonder at the look of fear in her eyes. Had she never held a *boppli* before? She'd looked upon Adam as though he was a poisonous snake rather than an innocent *boppli*, and that concerned Samuel.

In the kitchen, Lila placed a second batch of yeast rolls in the basket and covered them with the linen towel to keep them warm.

Rachel entered the kitchen and watched her for a moment. "Are you alright, Lila? You seem to be a little nervous. Was it too much for you to prepare the meal for this many people? I know you're not used to this much cooking."

"*Nee,* we don't have this much *familye* back in Nappanee. Most of them are scattered in other communities."

Rachel felt compassion tug at her heart. "I'm certain your *onkel* would enjoy it if you stayed on here at the B&B for a while."

"I will be settling here, it seems. A letter arrived today with the details. *Mei daed* has finally managed to sell *Onkel* Jessup's farm for him, and he will be here in three weeks. We will live in the *dawdi haus. Onkel* has asked me to clean and paint it to prepare for his arrival."

Rachel pulled Lila into an unexpected hug. "That's *wunderbaar!"*

Lila turned serious. "I promise it won't interfere with the wedding preparations you've asked for my help with."

"I'm not so much worried about that as I am with you taking on another project on your own. You seem so stressed as it is."

Lila waved her off. "I will be able to get everything done as long as there are no guests at the B&B."

Rachel smiled thoughtfully. "I will ask Samuel to help you. He enjoys painting."

"*Nee,*" Lila said with an urgency that alarmed Rachel.

She patted Lila's arm. "I know you aren't used to *familye* helping, but my *familye* does nothing but help each other. I'm certain it will be no trouble at all for Samuel to help you get the *dawdi haus* ready for your *daed.*"

Lila smiled nervously as she thanked Rachel. How was she going to endure being alone with Samuel while they painted the *dawdi haus?* She would just have to spend more time in prayer asking *Gott* for strength to resist the temptation that Samuel posed.

Lila returned to the dining room and took her place across from Samuel. She could feel his eyes on her, and it made her too nervous to finish her meal. Pushing the potatoes and asparagus around on her plate, Lila decided to focus on the banter around the long table.

"We must finish the fitting of your dress," Lizzie said to her *dochder*. "You have to take a little time off from the bakery to let me sew it, or it will not be finished in time for the wedding."

Katie nudged her. "I'd be more than happy to take over for a day if you need me to. We can't have the bride showing up to her own wedding in an old work dress."

Rachel's eyebrows furrowed. "That's *narrish*, Katie. You are too close to term. I can't have you giving birth to *mei bruder's boppli* in the bakery."

"If *Onkel* can do without me for the day," Lila said cautiously. "I'd be more than happy to step in for you."

"I thought you were going to spend the day painting the *dawdi haus*, Lila," Bess interjected.

"I'd be more than happy to help you paint, Lila," Samuel offered.

Rachel smirked at her *bruder*. "I already volunteered you for the job, Samuel."

Lila's cheeks heated up, and she could feel Samuel's gaze upon her once more. She resisted the urge to make eye-contact with him, no matter how tempting it was to get lost in the sea of blue in his eyes that lured her in like a fish. It was best if she not give him any reason to hope they could be anything more than distant acquaintances. She was not the one for him. She was certain he deserved more than she could offer even if she was interested—which she was not. That's the way it would remain as long as she had control over guarding her heart.

After the meal, all the women crowded into the kitchen to help with the cleanup, with the exception of Bess, who needed to nurse Adam and get him to sleep for a while. Lila could tell the *boppli* was draining the woman of her energy, but Bess remained smitten with her infant.

Katie sat at the small table in the kitchen, rolling her hand lovingly over her large belly as though her *boppli* were already born. Lizzie, Rachel, and Abby worked like machines to scrape plates, stack them, and put away all the messes Lila had made while she was cooking. Each worked, leaving Lila to put on a fresh pot of *kaffi* for the *menner,* who waited in the other room for shoofly pie. Lillian sat across from Katie at the table, bouncing one-year-old Ellie on her knee to keep her from fussing.

Lizzie handed her a wet dishcloth. "Let her chew on this. She needs something to bring those molars in. Poor thing must be in pain."

Lila felt a little out of sorts being in such an enclosed setting with Samuel's *familye.* They were *her familye* by marriage, but that didn't make her feel any closer to them. She hoped that in time she would get used to being around them. Since all her friends back home were married, she hadn't seen much of them and wasn't used to being around this many women all at once. They seemed to be enjoyable, and if it was possible, she might even become friends with them—but not with Samuel—definitely not with Samuel.

CHAPTER 8

Before long, Lila began to relax as she fell in step with the women in the kitchen. They all seemed to work in sync with one another, and Lila soon found her place wiping the dishes dry and replacing them in the cupboards. She was still learning her way around Bess's kitchen, and putting away dishes was a *gut* way to learn.

Rachel knocked elbows with Lila. "What do you think of *mei bruder,* Samuel?"

Lila nearly dropped the glass plate she was drying. What exactly was it that Rachel was asking her? "I don't know him," she answered simply.

Rachel smirked. "You don't know any of us yet, but it seems like you were avoiding Samuel most of the night. He was trying hard to get your attention."

Lila didn't dare say a word as she took the next clean plate from Lizzie to dry. She didn't want to discuss what she thought of Samuel in front of his *mamm*.

"Rachel, don't embarrass the poor girl," Lizzie said over her shoulder.

"We have been trying to get Samuel matched up with someone for a while, and he keeps turning them away," Katie said from where she sat at the table with Lillian.

"It seems he wants to be a bachelor for the rest of his life," Lillian added.

What did all of this have to do with her? Lila didn't want to be part of this conversation. She didn't want to paired up with Samuel, and if that's what these women were up to, she didn't want anything to do with them.

"There is nothing wrong with a *mann* wanting to be a bachelor," Lila stated nervously.

Rachel took the next plate, leaving Lila with nothing to busy her nervous hands. "I think he wants to be married, but he just hasn't found the right girl yet."

"I noticed him watching you several times throughout the meal, Lila" Katie interjected.

Lillian smiled. "I noticed the same thing."

"I think we all did," Abby said.

Lila didn't find anything too amusing about this conversation, but Samuel's *familye* seemed to be having fun at her expense.

She stiffened her upper lip. "I hadn't noticed him watching me, and if I had, I probably would have politely asked him to stop."

Rachel giggled. "You could tell him to stop, but I doubt he would. He was swooning over you."

The women in the room all laughed, and Lila pasted on a smile to keep from letting them know the subject of Samuel was not one she cared to talk about.

"If he was swooning, he was alone in it, because I have no interest in him." Lila tried to keep an even tone to prevent them from seeing how disturbed she was by the conversation.

"Not even a little?" Katie asked. "He's a handsome young *mann.*"

"And thoughtful, too," Abby chimed in. "And I'm not just saying that because he's *mei bruder.*"

"And he's available," Lillian added.

Lila's lips narrowed to a grim line. "Well I'm not—available."

The women looked at each other and turned serious. Had she ended the conversation, or had she merely insulted them and their efforts to help her?

"So you have a beau back in Nappanee?" Katie finally asked.

"*Nee,* I don't have a beau," Lila said quietly.

Lizzie turned around from the sink after washing the last dish. "Are you married, then?"

Lila was getting tired of all the personal questions. "*Nee,* I'm not married, and I don't intend to ever marry."

Abby placed a comforting hand on Lila's shoulder. "You poor thing; you've had your heart broken."

If having your *mamm* die just after giving birth to you, and growing up without a *mamm* while everyone around you has one, then, yes, her heart had been broken beyond repair. But she was certain they were talking about heartbreak from a beau.

"*Nee,* I've never even dated before," Lila said, her face heating from the confession.

She didn't want them to know her deepest secrets, but they were prying them out of her.

Lizzie suddenly shooed the other women from the room.

"Why do *we* have to leave?" Abby asked. "What did we do? We were just trying to get to know Lila a little better!"

Lizzie looked at Lila, who was shaking.

"I think you've asked enough questions for now. Give us a minute to talk. *Git* on out of here—all of you," Lizzie said with an authoritative tone.

After they shuffled from the kitchen one-by-one, Lizzie invited Lila to sit at the table with her. She placed a hand on Lila's from across the table.

"I understand from Jessup that you grew up without a *mamm.* I'm sure that's been tough on you, since most girls see an older sibling dating, or they talk to their *mamm* about such things. If you ever want to talk, you can talk to me or *mei Aenti* Bess, or any of these women. We are *familye* now, and we want you to feel like you can come to us if you need to."

Lila appreciated Lizzie's kindness, but she didn't think the woman understood her situation.

"*Mei mamm* died a few minutes after giving birth to me, I don't want to put a child through that. So I made a choice not to marry or have any *kinner.*"

Lizzie became serious. "I grew up without a *mamm* too. It wasn't like your situation; she was with me until I was ten years old. But sometimes I think that was harder on me because I got the chance to become attached to her. That may sound like a harsh thing to say, but it's sometimes easier to deal with a loss we never knew than to love someone that long and lose them. But you can't let that situation rule your entire life. You're young and full of life. I understand your fear, but that doesn't mean you should be alone for the rest of your life. Nothing in this world is guaranteed, but that doesn't mean we should close ourselves off to the possibilities *Gott* has in store for us."

Lila felt the need to make Lizzie understand, hoping she would let the matter drop. "I'm afraid the same thing will happen to me, and I will leave a *boppli* without a *mamm*. I know *mei mamm* didn't do it on purpose to me, but she still did it." Lila knew that was a harsh thing to say, but it was how she felt.

Lizzie smiled warmly. "Don't let your fear of the unknown cause you to miss *Gott's* calling in your life—even if that calling involves marrying and having *kinner*."

CHAPTER 9

Lila was eager to begin painting the *dawdi haus,* but it was Sunday and everyone was out visiting. She felt anxious with nothing to do, but she knew better than to take on such a laborious task on the day of rest. She'd prepared the meal ahead of time in anticipation for Jessup and Bess to return, but even that hadn't occupied enough of her day. *Onkel* had invited her to go with them, but she didn't want to chance running into Samuel. She'd had enough of his charm last night at dinner, and she wasn't certain she could continue to reject him if she didn't try to avoid him altogether. Lila had never felt such temptation from any other before Samuel, and she wasn't sure what made him so different from the others.

Lila pulled her cloak around her shoulders to shelter her from the wind and walked out to the dock out back of the B&B. The sun peaked around from the clouds, but it wasn't enough to warm her. A cold wind blew across the large pond, rippling the surface. Except for the wind, it was quiet, lacking the usual sounds that summer provided. It had turned too cold for the frogs and crickets. Even the fireflies and mosquitoes had long-since gone for the season. The trees clung to the last of their leaves of autumn-rich hues, a tell-tale sign that winter was on its way.

Lowering herself at the end of the dock, she folded her legs under her rather than dangling them over the edge. She wished it was warmer so she could dip her feet in the water, but the icy wind coming off the oversized pond was enough to discourage the temptation. Despite the cold that tried to chill her bones, it was a very peaceful, pleasant afternoon. She was grateful for the day away from everyone so she could finally take some time to think.

"I see you found my favorite thinking spot," a now-familiar baritone voice interrupted her reverie.

Looking up into the sinking sun, she spotted Samuel making his way to end of the dock. Her heart tumbled behind her ribcage as she admired the way the sun lit up his strong features. His broad shoulders looked somehow wider with the sun behind him, and the chisel of his jaw peppered by a day's growth of whiskers, gave him a more rugged look. Why couldn't he just leave her alone? Why did he have to stir feelings in her that she was trying to push down?

Lila lifted slightly off the end of the dock and looked at the worn planks of wood beneath her. "I don't see your name on this spot."

She didn't mean to react in such a snotty tone, but she wanted him to leave—or did she? The depth of his dimples as he smiled when he sat down beside her was enough to snatch the air from her lungs.

"I actually wrote it here when I was younger, but it has worn off since then," he said smoothly. "But everyone knows this is my spot."

He smiled again, bringing heat to her cheeks.

"It's surprisingly cold today, but I suppose that is to be expected now that it's the end of October. Are you warm enough?"

A gust of wind caused her teeth to chatter. "*Jah,*" she said through clenched teeth.

Before she realized, Samuel had shrugged off his wool coat and was placing it around her shoulders. His warm hands brought shivers to her as they brushed her neck. What was happening to her? His charming pull was interrupting her every thought; every reasonable argument she had for getting up and leaving immediately was thwarted by the lingering warmth of his touch.

Attempting to summon the strength to leave, she tried to wriggle from his coat, but she couldn't help but breathe in the smell of straw and horses, along with the rugged smell of shaving soap that clung to the collar. How would she be able to resist this *mann* if she didn't stop acting so foolishly? She was normally so strong-willed, but his kindness had broken through the barrier of her heart, and it seemed to take up residence there.

"Perhaps since I will be living here from now on, I should put *my* name at the end of the dock so there will be no more confusion," Lila said lightly.

She was surprised she was even able to form a coherent sentence with the smell of this handsome *mann* filling her senses.

Samuel plucked a pen from his shirt pocket and wrote her name beside her before she even had a chance to stop him.

"I was kidding," she said, trying not make to eye contact with him.

Then he wrote *his* name beside his leg, causing Lila to roll her eyes. Was he trying to impose on her space on purpose?

"Now it's *both* of our spot," he said as he replaced the pen in his pocket.

Lila met Samuel's gaze, and it was enough to warn her she did not have the strength to resist him. The blue in his eyes reflected the glint of the sinking sun over the water, and it was almost hypnotizing. If she didn't move quickly, she would be lost forever in their depths.

CHAPTER 10

Lila stood abruptly, easing Samuel's warm, masculine-scented coat from her shoulders. She tossed the coat in his lap, and a wind gust stole his scent from her, sending it floating across the pond.

"*Danki* for your kindness, but I have a meal to prepare for *Onkel's* return."

She did not dare meet his gaze, nor did she give him time to stop her, for her feet padded across the dock as swiftly as they could in a lady-like manner.

When she reached the back door to the B&B, she stopped to catch her breath.

I have a plan for my life, and it does not include a husband or kinner. I will not give in to that mann's temptation to change my mind.

Lila knew she could tell herself that all day long and it was not going to matter. Samuel had already breached the wall that surrounded her heart, and that frightened her.

ঝেওন্ব

Samuel lifted his coat to his face, breathing in the lingering scent of homemade banana bread and coconut oil she probably used to smooth her hair back. He knew his *schweschders* used it, but the scent of it never affected him like it did now, knowing it belonged to Lila. He was beside himself with worry over why she resisted his attempts to befriend her.

Lift the burden that rests on Lila's shoulders, Gott, and shelter her under your wing.

Samuel's gaze fell upon the ripples in the water that moved across the pond. Was it possible that he already loved Lila? If he did, he feared she would never love him in return. He thought he'd seen a flicker of hope in her startling green eyes, but it left as soon as he'd recognized it. What was she hiding from him that held such defenses against her heart? Had another *mann* broken her heart by ending an engagement to her? He couldn't imagine any *mann* doing such a thing to her. He could only hope that there was an easier explanation.

ঝেওন্ব

At the evening meal, Lila was not surprised to see Samuel at the table with Bess and *Onkel*

Jessup. Samuel had agreed to help *Onkel* put up storm windows on the B&B to prepare for winter, and Lila had overheard her *onkel* invite him to partake in the meal with them. She didn't want to sit with Samuel through another meal, but she was grateful that Bess and Jessup would be there to filter his interaction with her.

Lila stood at the stove pouring brown gravy into a serving bowl when she heard the back door open. Samuel's masculine scent drifted to her nose with the gust of wind that entered the door with him. She immediately felt her stomach tighten anxiously. Samuel was early, and *Onkel* was busy helping Bess put Adam down so she could eat with them. She didn't dare turn around when he greeted her; she knew that if she looked into his sparkling blue eyes she might not survive the temptation to get lost there.

Be strong. It's only one meal. Resist him until Onkel and Bess finish, and there will be nothing to worry about.

Lila could hear Adam fussing from the other room, as his parents tried to soothe him. If they couldn't get him to settle down, she feared she would be forced to entertain Samuel until they finished with the *boppli*. Lila continued to busy herself preparing the meal and completely ignored Samuel.

Before long, Adam's fussing turned to wailing. Lila glanced at Samuel looking for a sign that the crying was normal. She'd never heard a *boppli* cry so hard, but she'd never spent too much time around any to fully compare.

Just when Lila didn't think she could stand the screaming any longer, *Onkel* entered the kitchen, desperation showing in the lines of his face.

"Samuel, please call the doctor. I think something is wrong with *mei buwe.*"

"I saw his buggy at the Beiler farm on my way over here," Samuel said. "I'll fetch him at once."

With that, Samuel was out the door, and Jessup disappeared. Lila heard the bedroom door open and close, muffling Adam's screams once again. Lila returned the food to the stove, placing it back in the pots and pans to keep it warm. Filling the sink with sudsy water, Lila began to wash the dirtied dishes to keep her hands busy.

Dear Gott, please spare the boppli from whatever pain he's in. Bring the doctor swiftly, and bless him with the ability to assess Adam's condition. Heal that innocent boppli, and don't take him away from his mamm and daed.

Lila tried to keep her mind off the cries that did not subside from the upstairs room. She tried not to think about what could happen, but she knew it was another reason she did not want to bring a *boppli* into the world. Too many things could go wrong that could take a *mamm* away from a *boppli,* or the other way around. Panic raced through her at the thought of Bess losing her *boppli.*

Tears fell unchecked from Lila's chin dropping into the dishwater. She mindlessly washed the dishes until Samuel threw open the kitchen door. Startled, Lila pulled her apron to her face and wiped away evidence of her distress over the situation. It was too late. Doctor Davis followed the sound of Adam's screams while Samuel approached Lila, laying a comforting hand on her shoulder.

"He's going to be fine," Samuel said, his smooth baritone voice sending shivers through her.

His nearness paralyzed, her and his scent charmed her into submission. She felt a strong pull toward him, feeling like she couldn't resist him if he were to pull her into his strong arms and hold her captive against the strong plane of his chest. Could it really be that simple to let him comfort her?

Gott, give me the strength to resist this mann.

It was no use; she allowed herself to drift toward him as he encompassed her in the safety of his embrace.

CHAPTER 11

Lila flinched away from Samuel. She had to be stronger than the pull she felt from this *mann*. It would take extreme measures to guard her heart from him, but she would not let him pull her into a dream that could never be hers. How could she have given in to such a moment of weakness? She didn't want him to think she was interested in him. The feel of his embrace haunted her, enticing her to allow more of the same.

"You don't always have to be so strong and independent," Samuel said.

It would be too easy for her drift back into his arms, but she'd made a choice for her life, and she had no intention of changing her mind.

"Maybe I do."

Lila suddenly realized the *boppli* had stopped crying. Alarm caught in her throat where it nearly choked her with emotion. Samuel drew her back to him, and she didn't resist the peaceful retreat his strong arms offered. She breathed him in, wishing she could shut out the world and all the hurt that came with it. Blinking away fresh tears, Lila felt safe in the clutches of Samuel's arms. She reasoned with herself that she would bask in the safety of his affections, but she would not allow herself to lose herself in him.

An upstairs door opened and Lila pulled away at the sound of footfalls padding down the steps. She couldn't read the doctor's face to discover the outcome of the visit with Bess's *boppli*.

Gott, please let him be alright.

Doctor Davis sighed. "Just a bad case of colic." He sniffed toward the food warming on the stove. "Do you have enough to spare this old man some supper? I'm afraid by the time I reach home the missus will have already eaten."

Lila snapped into action. "*Jah.* Sit. I'll make you a plate."

Out of the corner of her eye, Lila could see Samuel sit down across from the doctor at the table in the kitchen. Now she would have to serve him as well. Otherwise the doctor might find her impertinent. She readied two plates and served the *menner* who sat making small-talk about the weather.

"Thank you, dear child," Doctor Davis said with a worn smile on his aging face. "Won't you sit down and join us?"

Samuel nodded, his dimples showing as he winked at her.

Lila's heart thumped an extra beat. "*Nee,* I should wait for *Onkel* and Bess."

The doctor put his fork down and wiped his mouth. "You might want to eat without them. That baby wore them out. They thought it was best if they rested now that he's settled down. I don't think they'll be joining us anytime soon."

Samuel jutted his chin out toward the food on the stove. "Get a plate and join us."

"Might as well eat it while it's hot," the doctor said. "You should be the one enjoying your cooking. It's very good. You'll make some young man a good wife with cooking this good."

The doctor's comment struck a nerve, and it didn't help that Samuel smiled at her as if to say he'd like to have her as his *fraa.*

"Will you excuse me, please?"

Lila dashed to the back door, grabbed her cloak off the peg on the wall, and shouldered her way out into the cold night. She padded across the back yard to the dock and didn't stop until she reached the end. Her breath created steam that showed bright against the moonlight. It was cold, and her teeth chattered, but she didn't care. Anything was better than being paired off like cattle. Lila didn't like being teased, especially about something she was so much against. Did everyone really expect her to get married? Why did it seem that was her only choice?

In the crisp, stillness of the night, Lila could hear the back door to the B&B open. She hoped it was only the doctor leaving to go back home, but she knew the old *mann* would stay until he finished his meal. That only left one other person that would walk out that door; Samuel.

Lila turned around to face him as he sauntered up the dock toward her. His chiseled features were illuminated in the moonlight, the depth of his dimples looking like the dark side of the moon. He was too handsome to resist, and his confidence made him even more appealing. How was she to resist Samuel if he was always around? It almost seemed that everyone expected them to pair up, and she would have no say in the matter. It wasn't fair that as an Amish woman, it was assumed she would marry and have lots of *kinner*. What about what *she* wanted? Didn't that matter?

Samuel closed the space between them and placed his wool coat around her shoulders. The sweet memory of his arms around her when they were in the kitchen taunted her. Was there somewhere deep in her subconscious that wanted what he offered? She had enjoyed the closeness between them so much it frightened her. She had a plan for her life, and now she felt confused all because of one embrace. An embrace that left her wanting something she thought she would never want.

Why did he have to be so wonderful and irresistible? Why couldn't he be more like Henry

Hochstetler from back home? Then she could just be content with being his friend. It was because Samuel was nothing like Henry. Samuel was handsome and kind the same as Henry, but Samuel was just a little bit too confident. That smooth confidence both scared *and* angered her.

"I don't want to marry you," Lila blurted out.

Samuel smirked at her. "I don't remember asking you!"

CHAPTER 12

Lila glared at Samuel, but he could see in her eyes that she was upset by his comment.

"So you don't want to marry me?" she asked through pursed lips.

Samuel found it hard to keep from laughing. Lila was on his hook, and she didn't even realize it. How long would he keep her dangling there before cutting her loose or reeling her in?

"I didn't say I didn't want to marry you, but I didn't ask you, either."

He smiled so brightly, the moon was pale in comparison. Lila turned her gaze toward the pond to keep from falling prey to the lure of his charming arrogance.

"Did you want me to ask you?" Samuel quipped.

Lila hesitated.

What was she waiting for? The anticipation rolling through Samuel's veins was enough to set his nerves ablaze. Did she want to marry him? He knew he already liked her, but was he ready to ask her to marry him?

Pursing her lips, Lila jutted her chin out. What was wrong with her? She knew the answer to that question just as sure as she knew her own name. But for the first time, she was unsure of the decision she'd made so long ago. Now that the question was actually being posed, she didn't have the heart to turn Samuel away. What was happening to her?

"I don't want you to ask me," she said soberly.

Lila slipped out of the warmth of Samuel's coat and handed it to him. She tried to walk past him, but he stopped her and pulled her into his arms. Caught off guard, Lila didn't fight him when he lowered his lips to hers. His warm breath quieted the echoes of reason her mind stirred to the surface.

Heat radiated off Samuel, scorching her with desire for him. Lila deepened the kiss like a woman who was ready to commit her heart and soul to him. But was she really prepared to marry him simply because of his magnetic pull on her heart? Lila was falling for him, no doubt, but her mind told her to back away before it was too late—if it wasn't already.

Samuel curled his fingers around the nape of Lila's neck, drawing her closer still. He couldn't help himself. He wanted to drink her in like she was the last drop of water in an acrid desert. His heart was already bestowed to her whether she was ready for it or not. Her mouth had said she didn't want him, but her lips against his told him she did.

"Marry me," he whispered at her temple.

"I can't," she whispered as her lips dragged across his rugged cheek until they met his once more.

Samuel cupped her cheeks in his hands and deepened the kiss. He would either wear her down with his fervent kisses, or he would enjoy it as long as she would allow it. Either way, he wasn't willing to let her go without giving it everything he had. Something about her made him want her for his *fraa* when he'd never even given marriage a single thought before.

"Marry me, Lila" he whispered again.

Lila's heart did a flip flop in her chest. Why did Samuel have to be so handsome and such a *gut* kisser? If he wasn't so wonderful, she would have no trouble resisting him at all, but she had to do it. Her fear of the future wouldn't let go of the stronghold it had on her.

Lila broke away from Samuel and gazed into his eyes that reflected the harvest moon. How could she say no to him? She wanted to kiss him for the rest of her life, but she didn't want to make *bopplies* with him—or with any *mann*. He would expect to have *kinner,* and she wouldn't give them to him. It would break his heart more than if she let him go now while his feelings for her were still so new.

"I can't marry you, Samuel." She nearly choked on the words.

Lila watched Samuel's expression twist with sorrow, his eyes glazed over with emotion. Her stomach clenched with immediate regret.

"Why did you kiss me like that, then?"

"I could kiss you for the rest of my life, but that doesn't mean I can marry you."

Tension claimed Samuel's jaw. "Did I do something wrong? Was this too fast for you?"

"You did nothing wrong. I enjoyed kissing you, but you could wait a year and it wouldn't matter. I don't want to get married."

Samuel tried to pull her back into his arms, but the spell between them had broken. "I'll wait however long I have to."

Lila's eyes filled with tears. "Don't wait. It wouldn't be fair to you because I will never say yes."

He nodded grimly.

Lila knew she'd hurt him, but it was better to do it now than to wait until he'd vested too much of his heart. The cold no longer affected her, for her emotions numbed her from the inside out. She hated to leave him, but she knew that if she didn't leave now she never would. Staying would only hurt him more in the end.

Samuel let go of Lila. It was no use trying to keep her close to him if she didn't want to be there.

She glanced at him once more before walking away slowly. He could see she hadn't wanted to leave any more than he wanted her to go. Was this the part where he was supposed to go after her? He couldn't help but hope it was worth a try.

Sprinting across the wet grass, Samuel captured her up into his arms, catching her off guard. He pressed his lips to hers again, hoping she wouldn't resist him.

She didn't.

Pausing between kisses, he gazed into her fiery green eyes. "Don't marry me."

"What are you talking about?" she asked.

His look turned serious. "Don't marry me, then. Just kiss me every day for the rest of your life."

CHAPTER 13

"*Nee*, Katie, please wait until the doctor gets here!"

"I trust you," Katie said breathlessly. "You did a *gut* job of helping Bess to birth Adam."

Katie let out a scream from the pain. She pulled on the sleeve of Rachel's dress. "Please don't leave me. I'm scared. What if Caleb doesn't make it here on time?"

I've got to stop visiting pregnant women!

Rachel was trying not to show concern, not wanting to alert her *bruder's fraa*. "Let's concentrate of getting you comfortable first. Then we will worry about Caleb. The important thing is help you relax so that maybe you can keep from pushing until the doctor gets here."

Rachel had no idea why she was so nervous. She'd just been through this with Bess. But that day

she'd had no time to think about it. Now that she'd
had time to think about it, she didn't want to be in
this situation again—especially not with her
bruder's boppli.

"I called the doc from the barn, and he
should be here soon. Please try to wait until he gets
here."

Katie was not listening. Rachel could see that
the woman was already bearing down. She let out
another scream. Bess had not made this much fuss,
and Rachel feared something could be wrong.

Mopping up sweat from Katie's hair, Rachel
soothed her through a difficult, long contraction.

"It's getting worse," Katie cried. "I have to
get up. I can't lie in this bed anymore. It hurts my
back too much."

Rachel assisted Katie out of the bed and
helped her lean over the mattress. She rubbed her
lower back during the next contraction, and that
seemed to ease the pains. Rachel hoped that meant
it was Katie's position on the bed that had made her
so uncomfortable.

Grabbing a pillow and hugging it to her
chest, Katie leaned into the mattress during the next
contraction. They were coming faster and lasting
longer, and Rachel knew that meant it wouldn't be
long before she was ready.

With a sudden gush, Katie's water broke,
causing her to let out a scream with the pain of the
contraction. Rachel grabbed a few towels she'd

brought into the room with her and placed them around Katie's feet.

"I think I better get back in bed now," Katie said breathlessly.

Rachel agreed, helping her. She placed a clean towel beneath her and propped the pillows up behind her head just in time for the next contraction.

"I think you better catch *mei boppli,* Rachel."

A quick glance out the bedroom window showed no sign of the doctor or her *bruder,* so Rachel braced herself to catch Katie's *boppli.* One more contraction later the *boppli* was crowing.

"Push slowly, Katie, on the next contraction," Rachel urged her.

"I'll try," Katie squeezed out before pushing.

"It's a boy!" Rachel said around the lump in her throat.

Katie's eyes welled up with emotion as she reached for her new *boppli.* "Your *daed* will be so happy to see you," she cooed to him.

Rachel brought the quilt across Katie's lap to wait for the doctor to finish. "Where can I find a pair of scissors to cut the cord?"

Katie pointed to a sewing box in the corner of the room, her eyes not leaving her new son.

Rachel worked fast to tie and cut the cord.

"He's beautiful."

Katie looked up for only a moment. "*Danki.* For being here and helping me. I could not have done this without your help."

Rachel placed a warm hand on Katie's shoulder as she gazed upon the new life she'd helped bring into her *bruder's familye.*

"Do you have a quilt made for him?"

"Jah, it's in the cedar chest at the end of the bed." Katie pointed to a hand-carved piece of furniture she could see had been made by her *bruder.*

She lifted the lid and retrieved a small blue and yellow quilt and brought it to Katie so she could wrap her new *boppli* in it. Hearing faint buggy wheels, Rachel was relieved when she peered out the window at Caleb's buggy coming up the lane followed by Doctor Davis.

Rachel busied herself mopping up the floor, tossing the wet towels over the edge of the bathtub in the bathroom down the hall. When she returned to the room, Caleb was taking the stairs two at a time to get to Katie.

Joy filled his face as Caleb rushed to Katie's side. "Why didn't you wait for me?"

"Your son had other plans for his day," Katie said proudly.

Caleb's face lit with emotion. "It's a *buwe?"*

"Jah, and your *schweschder* helped deliver him."

Caleb looked at Rachel, who readied a pan of water and linens on the bureau across the room. His *thank you* showed in his misty expression without even saying a word to her. She smiled at her older *bruder,* feeling equally happy.

Doctor Davis entered the room and looked directly at Rachel. "Did you deliver this one, too?"

Rachel beamed. "*Jah,* but I didn't do it on purpose any more than I did with Bess."

"I'm glad you were here," Caleb said.

"I am too," Katie said, not looking up from her son.

"That makes three of us," Doctor Davis agreed.

Rachel offered a silent prayer for the miraculous outcome for the second time in the span of a week. If this kept up, she'd be known as the midwife of the community, and she wasn't certain she wanted the women in the community to start asking for her when they were birthing. She was more than happy to leave that task to the doctor. He was older and had more experience. Rachel only wanted to concentrate on her wedding for now.

Doctor Davis busied himself with examining the new *boppli.*

"He's healthy and strong, Caleb. Have you picked out a name?"

A few whispers later, and Caleb announced his new son, Isaac.

CHAPTER 14

Lila opened the windows to the *dawdi haus,* hoping it would air out quickly. After being closed up for several years without occupancy, the house needed a thorough cleaning, painting, and some airing out before it would be livable again. Once upon a time, Bess had used it as living space until she had the private living quarters sectioned off in the B&B. It seemed a shame to Lila that Bess had let the *haus* sit for so long as she looked around at the quaint little bungalow. It would be just the right size for her and her *daed.*

"It's a little stuffy in here."

Samuel's familiar baritone voice startled her. He advanced toward her and placed a quick kiss upon her cheek before setting down a bucket full of paint supplies. She watched him move about the small rooms assessing the needed repairs.

"It won't take much to get this place in order before your *daed* arrives."

Samuel's smile warmed her in the chilly *haus*. Had she made the right decision about their relationship? She wondered how long he would *really* be satisfied with things the way they were; sooner or later he would most likely want to marry her. Today, she decided, was not the day to think about that. She had work to do to prepare for her *daed's* arrival, and she was not about to let him down.

Lila surveyed the workspace. "I figured we should leave the linens on the furniture until we get the walls painted. I figured I could help with the painting since I can't do a lot of cleaning until it's finished."

Samuel smiled, his dimples tempting her to forget the painting and spend the day kissing him. But that would be neither practical nor advisable since she still wasn't certain if that was one of her best decisions.

"I'm just happy that today is a little warmer than it was yesterday so we can leave the windows open. It'll make the paint dry faster."

Lila pulled on the sleeves of her sweater. "It's still cold."

Samuel closed the space between them and drew her into his arms. "Is that better?"

Lila had to admit it was, but it wasn't going to get the work done. "*Jah,* but we have work to get done."

She pushed him away playfully. If she wasn't careful, she was going to fall in love with Samuel, and that was the last thing Lila planned on doing.

"*Mei bruder,* Caleb, and his *fraa,* Katie, had their *boppli* yesterday. Would you like to go with me to visit them?"

Lila's heart did a flip-flop. Forget her worry over falling in love with Samuel; seeing another *boppli* was the last thing she planned to do.

"*Nee,* I have too much to do. Besides, what if Bess needs my help." Lila knew it was an excuse, but Samuel didn't need to know she would never help Bess with her new *boppli.* But how long could she expect to keep such a secret from him?

Samuel pulled on Lila playfully, keeping her close to him. "So wouldn't you want a little place like this of your own someday?"

"I couldn't live on my own, Silly," Lila said.

Samuel pulled her into his arms again. "I meant with me."

Lila pushed him away again. "I already told you I'm not marrying you."

Samuel knelt down beside a can of white paint and used a key to open it. "I was hoping you might change your mind."

Lila was afraid of that. He was going to keep hoping until he either gave up or spent every day trying to wear her down. Either way, all she saw was heartbreak waiting at the end for both of them. How long could they be content with just kissing before they wanted more? She already wanted more, and her stomach was in knots just thinking about it.

"I can't, Samuel, and if you are going to continue to ask me, then the agreement we already have between us will never work."

Samuel poured paint in a plastic pan and closed the lid on the can. "Don't you think people will expect something to come of our relationship? What will we tell them?"

Lila picked up a paintbrush, dipped it in the paint, and brushed against the wall. "We will tell them it's none of their business. In my opinion, people are way too nosey as it is. They think they need to know everything about you. Maybe some things are too private for everyone else to know."

Samuel stroked the paintbrush along the opposite wall. "You won't hear any argument out of me there. *Mei schweschders* talk about a lot of stuff that I don't think is any of their business."

Lila giggled. It was the first time Samuel had heard her laugh and he liked it.

"Does this mean we are keeping our friendship a secret?"

"We are more than friends, and I think you know that." Samuel threatened to dab his paintbrush on her nose, but she backed away and squealed.

"I know nothing of the sort." Lila swiped her paintbrush across Samuel's cheek in jest.

Shaking his paintbrush toward Lila, Samuel watched her expression twist as paint splattered across the front of her, some on her face. Lila charged at him with her dripping brush, but he caught her in his clutches. She struggled to swipe at him with the paintbrush until he managed to take it from her and toss it on the drop-cloth on the floor.

"You don't play fair," Lila squealed. "You're stronger than I am."

"Just remember that when you keep turning down my proposals. I can hold out longer than you can."

"Sounds like you're challenging me," she giggled.

Samuel drank in the sound of her laughter.

"You won't turn me down forever."

His mouth captured hers as he pulled her closer. Samuel could get used to kissing her every day; that he was certain of.

CHAPTER 15

"Blake Monroe, where are you taking me?"

Rachel knew he was surprising her with a first look at the completed farm in which they would live once they wed, but she allowed him to think she hadn't a clue of his surprise. She would play along until the last minute, knowing how important this day was to her betrothed.

Blake had worked hard over the past year trying to prepare for their future together. He'd used the reward money he'd shared with Abby to build a home for the two of them to share after their wedding.

After going through the baptismal classes and taking the baptism, Blake had become Amish and very much a part of the community. Most of the *menner* has assisted him at one time or another in building the *haus,* but he'd wanted to do the inside work on his own. Rachel had to admit she was indeed very excited to see what the finished product looked like.

Eagerness filled Rachel as they approached a fair-sized farm *haus* complete with a large barn.

"I had no idea you were going to build this much *haus*," Rachel said with surprise.

"I used the majority of the reward money, but I saved aside enough to get us through two years. I figured that would give us enough time to make the farm operational where we could pull in a reasonable profit and yield enough of a crop to support us too. Your grandfather was very generous to sell me all thirty acres of his land, and I want to put it to good use."

Rachel couldn't help but feel a swell of pride for Blake. "You thought of everything. You have a sound business sense."

Blake chuckled. "I can't take credit for that. If not for Hiram's guidance, along with several of the men in the community, I would have probably spent the entire thing on just the house alone. I had visions of living in a mansion!"

Rachel sighed at the beauty of *grossdaddi's* property that had become theirs, and the *haus* and barn that she would soon call her own. "We don't need a mansion. This is perfect for us."

Blake nudged her playfully. "It has a few extra bedrooms for *bopplies.*"

Rachel felt her cheeks warm as Blake helped her out of the buggy. Already, Rachel envisioned flowerbeds filled with colorful, fragrant blooms and the kitchen garden she would have out back between the *haus* and the barn. A fenced corral beside the barn was set up for the horses, and she could already hear the chickens that would cluck as they roamed the yard. She could almost taste the fresh eggs that she would cook in her own kitchen—her own kitchen. She liked the thought of that.

"Are we going to look inside today, or do you want to save that for after our wedding?"

Rachel looked at him quizzically. "You don't want me to see the inside? I thought you said it was finished."

Blake scooped her into his arms to shield her from the chilly wind. "I can't wait for you to see the inside of the house, but *Englisch* tradition dictates that I am to carry you over the threshold the night of our wedding."

Rachel giggled as she nuzzled Blake's neck to warm herself. "That sounds very romantic."

Blake smothered her cheek with kisses until his lips met hers. "Does this mean you want to observe an *Englisch* tradition and wait to see the inside until I can carry you over the threshold?"

Rachel didn't have to think about the sacrifices Blake had made for her. The *haus* and his baptism had been more than she could have ever asked for. And so for him, she would gladly wait and share an *Englisch* tradition with the *mann* she loved.

CHAPTER 16

"Lila, could I trouble you to watch Adam for me while I get cleaned up?" Bess asked. "I feel like I haven't had but one bath in the week since I've had him."

Lila's voice caught in her throat, and before she could make a reasonable excuse as to why she couldn't watch him, the woman had disappeared into the washroom. Panic seized Lila as she crept near the cradle where little Adam slept soundly. She'd only entered the room the change the bed linens, and now she wished she hadn't.

What would she do if the *boppli* stirred from his peaceful slumber? She'd never held a *boppli,* and she didn't know the first thing about how to pick him up without breaking him or dropping him.

She'd watched Rachel flop him around like a kitten, and she didn't think she could ever handle a *boppli* with such ease. Not to mention the fact that she wanted nothing to do with *bopplies.*

Still, his little gurgling noises enticed her to draw close to the cradle and observe him sleep. His tiny little fists rested above the top edge of the quilt that was tucked snuggly around his tiny frame. He seemed so perfect in every way as he let little wisps of air escape his tiny rosebud mouth. The magnetic pull to watch Adam sleep was more than Lila thought possible. She'd never been this close to a *boppli,* and she had to admit, it was easy to see how others might be so enamored with the wee one.

Lila tiptoed around the room, cringing every time a floorboard creaked. Setting about the task of stripping the bed, Lila was extra careful not to make any noise. She carefully tucked in the bottom sheet and placed the pillow slips onto the feather pillows. After partially unfolding the top sheet, she flicked it to spread across the surface of the double bed. The crack of the linen as it floated above the bed startled Adam, causing him to let out a loud cry.

"*Nee, nee,*" Lila said to the *boppli.* "I didn't mean to wake you. I promise I'll be quieter if you stop crying."

Adam wailed so loudly, he could not have heard Lila's pleas—even if he *could* understand her. She rocked the cradle, hoping it would quiet him, but it was no use. Panic nearly seized her at the thought of having to pick him up. If Bess returned from her shower and saw that Lila had not tended to Adam, she would be angry.

Gott please make him stop crying. I'm too afraid to pick him up. What if I accidently drop him?

Peace filled Lila as soon as she breathed the prayer. Instinctively, she placed a hand under the *boppli,* cradling his head and bottom, and lifted him carefully from the cradle. He was much lighter than she'd anticipated—no heavier than the Miller's puppies.

Drawing him into the crook of her arms, Lila delighted in his sweet smell. She lifted his tiny head to her nose and breathed in the most heavenly scent she'd ever come across. How could something she'd feared all her life be so *wunderbaar?*

Little Adam looked up at her with big blue eyes that broke through the hardness over Lila's heart. She nestled him closer, surprised at the emotions that put a lump in her throat. How could she have thought to deprive herself of such a feeling? Had her own *mamm* felt this way about her just before she'd died? Lila's *daed* had described the look on her *mamm's* face when she'd held her for the first time after giving birth—just minutes before she'd hemorrhaged and passed away. Suddenly, thoughts of her *mamm* didn't bring pain and anger to the surface of her emotions, for they were too overcrowded with the simple joy of having a *boppli* in her arms.

Lila breathed a silent prayer, thankful for the opportunity to experience such joy in something that had paralyzed her with fear for so many years. Even though Adam was not her *boppli,* her heart filled with love toward him—an emotion she never would have thought was possible. She hugged her little cousin close and kissed the top of his sweet smelling head. Laughter filled her at the delight that poured over her. For the first time in her life, she felt free from the bondage of fear that had held her captive for too long. It was a liberating feeling to let go of something that had nearly ruined her future. She prayed that it wasn't too late for her to change this part of her life around.

Tears filled Lila's eyes as she suddenly realized how much she desired marrying Samuel and having as many *bopplies* as *Gott* would bless them with. Eagerness to tell Samuel she'd marry him occupied her immediate thoughts. It would be tough waiting for him to propose again—especially since she'd begged him not to ask her again. Nervousness crowded her sudden joy, overwhelming her with worry that he would never say the words again.

Lila looked down into Adam's innocent face.

"I think I've made a mess of things," she cooed to him. "What will I do if he never asks me again?"

Fresh tears filled Lila's eyes turning her joy to sorrow.

CHAPTER 17

Rachel's hands trembled as she fingered the letter she pulled from the mailbox. The return address told her it had come from the prison, and she wondered why Bruce would write to her. She was aware of the recent letter Blake had received from his *daed,* but she wasn't certain she could stomach the words of the *mann* who had kidnapped her just over a year ago. She'd worked so hard to put the incident behind her, and now, as she held the letter penned by the *mann* who had nearly killed her betrothed, Rachel felt the old wounds breaking open again.

Walking up the lane from the main road where the line of mailboxes invited the *Englisch* world to invade the peacefulness of their seclusion, Rachel felt secure in the protection her *familye* provided and in knowing Bruce would not likely get out of prison until he was a very old *mann*. Still, the letter set her nerves on edge, and she contemplated disposing of the letter without opening it. Knowing it wouldn't be right to keep the letter from Blake, Rachel tucked the letter in her apron pocket and walked up to the *haus*.

Not yet ready to go inside, Rachel pulled her cloak tightly around her and sat in one of the rockers on the front porch. She looked out onto the lawn and the large oak tree with its long branches that canopied the circle driveway. Sunlight glinted off the orange and red leaves. The crisp, afternoon sky boasted fluffy clouds teased with a silver lining of rain, and Lila wondered if it would bring the season's first snow flurries. If not for the chill from the breeze, Rachel could easily snuggle up on the porch swing and take a catnap. She was exhausted from endless preparations for her upcoming wedding, but her emotions now caved with heaviness from the letter tucked away in her apron pocket.

Why had Bruce chosen now to reach out to her? She wished he'd waited to contact her until after they'd put the wedding and its business behind them. But would there ever be a *gut* time to receive news from the *mann* who'd caused her and Blake so much grief? If only she hadn't seen the letter. It was too late now, and she would not be able to hide her melancholy from Blake.

Gott, renew the forgiveness I have in my heart for Bruce Monroe. Prepare my heart to receive whatever is in his letter, and bless me with the strength to be able to endure it.

A warm breeze brushed Rachel's cheeks, making her shiver—not from the cold day, but from the unusual warmth her prayer brought. Still shaking, Rachel lifted the letter from her apron pocket and opened it. She was ready to face the words of the *mann* who had kidnapped her—with a heart full of forgiveness.

Dear Rachel,

It is with a heavy heart that I write this letter to you. I know I don't have any right to be asking any favors of you, but I need to know that you forgive me for what I did to hurt you last summer. I never meant to cause any harm to anyone. At the time, I was consumed with alcohol, and that can make a man do terrible things. I've had more than a year to sober up in jail, and I even started going to Bible study with the preacher and a few other inmates.

I am truly sorry for what happened. I don't know if I will ever be able to forgive myself for shooting my own flesh and blood, but I thank God every day he didn't die because of the hate I carried in my heart. Blake is everything to me, and I'm just sorry it took me so long to realize it.

I still don't really know how this forgiveness thing works, but my boy told me the Amish people are true forgivers. I have prayed that is true. I only wish I can someday experience the unconditional love that the two of you have for each other, and my son seems to have for me. He's told me he forgives me, but I have a hard time wrapping my head around such a thing—especially since I don't think I will ever be able to forgive myself for almost killing him and putting you in so much danger. I'm sorry for scaring you half to death that day.

Because of my actions, I will miss out on seeing the two of you get married, and seeing my grandchildren grow up. Truthfully, that hardly seems punishment enough for what I put the two of you through. Know that I will pray for you, and spend the rest of my days in repentance for what I've done.

Yours Truly,
Bruce Monroe

Tears dripped from Rachel's eyes onto the page. How could she begrudge the *mann* for his apology—especially if it was from his heart? The letter seemed genuine enough, but she still held a little distrust for him. She breathed a quick prayer asking for guidance. Then her answer came to her.

Rushing up the stairs to her room, Rachel grabbed a few sheets of paper and began to pen a letter to Bruce.

Mr. Monroe,
Although I cannot speak for my betrothed (your son), I forgive you for everything. I am happy to hear you have an interest in the Bible, for the

words will guide you on learning to forgive yourself. I believe it is important to do that, not for us, but for your own peace of mind. I wish you well. Feel free to stay in touch. Blake and I will keep you up to date on the developments in our familye throughout the years.

Sincerely,
Rachel Yoder (soon to be Monroe)

Rachel folded the letter, feeling light of heart, and finally ready to marry Blake. Now there would be no hindrance to their future happiness. She was finally free of the past, and it felt liberating.

CHAPTER 18

"I'd be more than happy to give you a ride over there to help *mei schweschder,* Rachel, with the pumpkin rolls. I know how important they are to her, and if you're late, which I suspect you will be if you walk, she will not be happy with you."

Lila looked into Samuel's serious, blue eyes.

"I appreciate the offer, but didn't you just come from there? I don't want to make you take the trip all over again."

Samuel smiled as he pulled her into his arms and placed a kiss across her cold lips. "You're already freezing. Think of how cold you'll be by the time you get there. I think today is colder than it was yesterday."

Lila was already shivering, and the shelter of his arms had warmed her more than it should. She'd been looking for the opportunity to allow Samuel to propose to her again, and the close quarters of his buggy and the time it would take to drive her to meet Rachel might be the perfect setting.

"I am running a little late since I've been helping Bess with the *boppli* all morning. *Danki*. I promised Rachel I'd get there a little early to help her pick the pumpkins."

Samuel pulled her into a tight squeeze and kissed her again just before helping her into his buggy. It would be her first buggy ride with a *mann,* and she had to admit she was a little nervous. She loved him, but she feared he would give up on her since they'd made a deal *not* to marry. Why had she acted in haste? She should have never said anything to him about it. But at the time, she had no intention of marrying him. How could she convey to him, without being too bold, that she was now ready?

Samuel grabbed the reins, slapped them gently across his gelding, and clicked his tongue to signal a command. The buggy lurched forward, causing Lila to grab onto Samuel for stability.

He tucked his arm around her, pulling her closer to his side. "I'll hold onto to you so you don't slosh around."

"*Danki,* I'm certain your *schweschder* would appreciate it if I showed up to help her with the wedding in one piece."

Samuel chuckled. "Is this your first wedding?"

"*Nee,* I've attended a couple of other weddings."

"Well, as much against weddings as you are, I thought you might have avoided them until now."

Lila's heart sank. How could she tell Samuel she was no longer against marriage—that she wanted to marry—him? He would think she was *narrish* for sure and for certain. She couldn't seem too eager and blurt it out or he would lose respect for her. Perhaps she could ease into the conversation and keep him there until he made another attempt to propose. The only problem was that he'd made a promise to her that he wouldn't ask her again.

"I'm warming up to the idea," Lila said. "Your *schweschder* seems to be happy about getting married."

"Well, you don't have to worry about that since you will never get married. And don't worry about me asking you again. I promised you I wouldn't, and I won't." Samuel teased her, hoping it would change her mind, and from the look on her face, it was working.

Lila sighed hopelessly. What had she done? Was there no undoing her mistake? Now he would never ask her. An entire lifetime of being a childless spinster stretched out before her as she envisioned her life without Samuel.

"Stop the buggy," Lila said abruptly.

Samuel pulled over to the side of the country lane near his *familye* home. "What's wrong?"

Lila was shaking. "I'm feeling a little too warm, and I think I want to walk the rest of the way."

She jumped from the buggy, and Samuel followed her. "At least kiss me before you go."

"You already got your kiss for the day," Lila said, choking back tears. "You kissed me before I got into the buggy."

Samuel closed the space between them. "That one didn't count. Your lips were cold. Now that you're warmed up, I'd like a *real* kiss."

Lila couldn't resist him, even if kissing him was all she would ever have with him. There would be no marriage or *bopplies* in her future because she had broken her own heart with her hasty decision. Now, it seemed, there would no undoing it.

Samuel pressed his lips to hers, his hunger for her more apparent with every sweep of his mouth across hers.

"I love you," she whispered in-between kisses.

Panic seized her when she realized she'd let the words slip from her tongue.

Samuel pulled away and looked at her, his eyes glazed over with emotion. "I love you too!"

Lila smiled delightfully as she pressed her lips to Samuel's. It wasn't a marriage proposal, but it was progress.

CHAPTER 19

Rachel stood at the edge of her *mamm's* kitchen garden surveying the last bits of vegetation. Except for a few squash, it had been pretty well picked over, and the stores of canned vegetables she and her *mamm* had put up for winter filled their pantry.

A sense of accomplishment filled her as she realized she was bringing a great deal more to her marriage than she'd originally thought. She knew Blake expected nothing from her other than her love for him, but she wanted to be able to provide for him just as much as he was doing for her. Come spring, she would be planting her own kitchen garden at her own *haus,* and she hoped they would be blessed with their first *boppli* within their first year of marriage. It was going to be a *wunderbaar* year; she could just feel it in the air. The letter from

Bruce had freed her in a way she never thought possible; his letter could not have come at a more perfect time.

The pumpkin patch was another thing altogether. Six long rows boasted enough pumpkins to make the pumpkin rolls for her wedding meal. Her *schweschder,* Abby, *Aenti* Lillian, and Lila would arrive soon to help make pumpkin rolls. Rachel intended to get the pumpkins picked and cleaned before they arrived so she would be ready since time was running low.

With only three more days until her wedding, Rachel was more anxious than ever to complete as many tasks as possible ahead of time. She hadn't spent more than five minutes alone with Blake in the past two days, and she was ready to be married.

Pushing the wheelbarrow down the row, Rachel selected each pumpkin carefully, knowing the ones that were the most ripe would be the easiest to work with, and the tastiest. She left several on the vines that were still a little green. Rachel knew they would use them to make pies later, but they would need to be picked before the first frost and stored in the cellar. Her *mamm* had already promised her she could have most of the remaining pumpkins to make pies for her first Christmas with Blake. She had so many firsts to look forward to she found it difficult to concentrate on what she was doing.

Pushing the full wheelbarrow toward the kitchen door, Rachel was surprised to see Lila show up with her *bruder,* Samuel. She'd thought they would make a *gut* match, but Lila seemed very apprehensive around him the last time she'd seen them together. Rachel wondered what had changed as she watched the two of them smile and converse as though they'd known each other all their lives. But there was something else she couldn't quite understand. They almost acted like they were courting. Was it possible they'd begun courting in secret?

Rachel approached her *bruder's* buggy carefully watching the interaction between him and Lila. "Why did you bring her so late, Samuel?"

Lila stepped forward, eyeing the wheelbarrow full of pumpkins near the back door to the *haus.* She couldn't detect from Rachel's mood if she was angry that she was too late to help with the picking. "I'm sorry, Rachel. It was my fault we were late."

Rachel planted her fists on her hips and eyed Samuel for an explanation.

Samuel tried to divert his *schweschder's* obvious annoyance with him. "Don't look at me like that. For a change, it wasn't any of my doing."

Lila leered at Samuel. "You don't have to blame it *all* on me!"

Samuel nudged her playfully. "I'm not the one who jumped out of the buggy."

Rachel's eyes grew wide. "You jumped out of his buggy?"

Samuel held up a hand. "It wasn't moving!"

Lila was suddenly angry at the blame Samuel was letting her take responsibility for. "I might have jumped out of the buggy, but you're the one who..." she suddenly realized what she was about to say, and stopped herself abruptly. She could feel the heat rising up her cheeks in a tell-tale hue.

Rachel gasped. "You kissed her!"

Samuel chuckled. "She kissed me back!"

Lila felt her face heat up, and anger took over her emotions. "It won't happen again!" she stormed off, leaving the two of them while she grabbed a pumpkin in each hand and walked inside the kitchen.

She was too angry with herself for nearly telling hers and Samuel's secret, but she was even more angry with him for actually revealing something so intimate between them. How would she ever be able to face Rachel again? Worse, how would she get through an afternoon of making pumpkin rolls with Samuel's relatives without being teased?

Before Lila could get her cloak off and hang it on a peg near the kitchen door, Rachel came bustling in the door toting a pair of pumpkins.

She looked at Lila sincerely. "I'm sorry for blurting that out. I was just so excited that *mei bruder* finally has someone. We've all been praying for him that he would find someone he could marry, but he hasn't even courted anyone yet."

Lila narrowed her mouth into a serious line.

"We aren't getting married."

Rachel's look softened. "Of course not right away, but I'm certain he will ask you."

Lila took the pumpkins from Rachel and put them on the table. "He already did—more than once."

Rachel tipped her head to the side quizzically.

"You don't want to marry Samuel?"

Emotions surfaced, bringing tears to Lila's eyes. "I do, but I told him I didn't."

Rachel looked at Lila affectionately. "Why?"

Lila felt unsure if she could confide something so personal with a woman she barely knew. But Rachel was not a stranger; she was Samuel's *schweschder*. Surely she could trust someone so close to the *mann* she loved.

"I didn't even tell Samuel the reason." Lila said quietly.

Rachel placed a comforting hand on Lila's shoulder. "You don't have to tell me if it's too personal. But I would encourage you to share it with *mei bruder*. I could see the love in his eyes for you already. I'd hate for his heart to get broken."

Lila felt the sting of reality hit her. She didn't want to break Samuel's heart any more than she wanted her own heart to break. Is that why he hadn't asked her again? Had she broken his heart a little? She hoped her declaration of love had smoothed that over and would open the door for a future proposal from him.

"Would you mind if I practice on you before I have to tell Samuel? I do owe him that, but I'm afraid."

Rachel offered an accepting smile. "Whatever it is, you can be certain he is a very understanding *mann*. I see in his eyes how much he loves you, and that will not change. But you need to be able to trust him with whatever is holding you back."

"I decided a long time ago that I didn't want to marry and have *kinner* because *mei mamm* died a few minutes after I was born. She only got to hold me for a minute, and then she hemorrhaged. The doctor was not there, and *mei daed* couldn't save her. I've spent my entire life being afraid of the same thing happening to me."

"But you said you changed your mind?" Rachel interrupted.

"*Jah,* when I held little Adam yesterday, I realized that the risk is worth the reward."

Rachel pulled Lila into a hug. "Then you need to share your change of heart with Samuel. He will ask you again—I'm certain of it."

Lila prayed she was right.

CHAPTER 20

Abby and Lizzie entered in through the already crowded kitchen at the Yoder home.

"Lillian isn't coming," Lizzie said. "Ellie had a stomach ache and she doesn't want you getting sick before the wedding."

Rachel felt disappointment at her *aenti's* absence, and worry for her cousin. But they had too much work to finish for her to spend time dwelling on something she had no control over. She whispered a prayer for her *familye* and then went back to work carving the meat from the pumpkins.

Lila placed a stew pot on the stove in preparation for cooking the pumpkin. She busied herself away from the others, feeling a little intimidated since they were all *familye*.

Rachel put her arm around Lila and pulled her back toward the table. "If we are to be *familye,*" she whispered. "You better get used to talking to us."

Lila felt her pulse quicken and her cheeks heat up with worry that the others had overheard Rachel's whispers. She smiled, putting her best face forward, and bit down her anxiety for Samuel's sake. Rachel was right about her needing to draw closer to his *familye*. It would give the probability of their future together a little push in the right direction. If she could get closer to these women, Samuel would be more likely to propose. Lila had not had the advantage of having *familye* around her. She usually avoided community gatherings since she and her *daed* had mostly closed themselves off from everyone. Her *daed* had never gotten over losing her *mamm,* and Lila shied away from social events for the same reason.

Maybe Rachel's advice was for her own *gut,* especially since she had never taken advantage of community events to draw her into the security and love they offered. Why *had* she closed herself off from everyone all these years? Now that she'd been exposed to the kindness and sense of belonging that *familye* offered, she was grateful for her *daed's* decision to send her here to stay with *Onkel* Jessup and her new *Aenti* Bess. Her new cousin, Adam, was going to grow up knowing he had *familye* that loved him; Lila would make sure of it.

Lila moved about the kitchen, aware of the closeness of these women, and couldn't help but want to be a part of Samuel's *familye.* He had declared his love for her only a few short moments before, and she was giddy with her love for him. It amazed her how much her life had changed since she'd come to stay in this community. Would her *daed* recognize the changes in her and want to change himself too? She hoped the move to be near his *bruder* would help him to be more social. They had both spent a lifetime of being lonely and cut off from loved-ones. It was time to put the past to rest along with her *mamm,* and move on with their lives.

"Let me help you with that," Lila said bravely as she took two pumpkins from Abby's arms. "You shouldn't be lifting these in your condition."

Abby giggled. "I'm hoping a little hard work will bring this *boppli* into the world. I feel like I've been pregnant for too long. But I know it is all in *Gott's* timing."

Lila placed a comforting hand on her shoulder as she offered her a chair at the table. "How much longer do you have?"

Abby blew out a breath as she sat down with difficulty. "It should be any day now. I can't believe *mei bruder,* Caleb and his *fraa,* Katie, had their *boppli* before I did. I've been married longer than they have."

Lila smiled. "Like you said; it's all in *Gott's* timing."

Abby patted Lila's hand. "You will make a *gut fraa* for *mei bruder,* Samuel."

Lila looked at Rachel. "Does everyone know?"

Lizzie crossed the room and pulled Lila into a hug. "I didn't know until just now. Why am I always the last to know what my *kinner* is up to?"

Lila swallowed hard. "I'm sorry you had to find out this way, but I'm not even certain I will be marrying Samuel. I'm waiting for him to ask me—again."

Lizzie pulled her coat off the peg near the door.

"I'm not sure I want to know what that is all about. I think you can let me know when it's official." She smiled at Lila. "Right now, I'm late to go meet *mei* new *grandkinner.*"

When she closed the door, Abby and Rachel giggled. "*Mamm* always thinks we keep things from her," Abby said.

"We do sometimes," Rachel said. "But she should expect that. It's the way *kinner* is. Our own *kinner* will do the same to us one day."

Abby rolled a hand over her large stomach.

"This *boppli* better not keep secrets from me."

Lila went to the stove and stirred the cooking pumpkin. She couldn't help but think that if she'd been fortunate enough to grow up with her *mamm* that she would have told her everything. She'd longed her entire life to tell her every little thing that happened to her. It was an especially large void now that she was in love and wanted to marry. It saddened her that her *mamm* would never have the chance to meet her *grandkinner*. Perhaps it was time she started sharing the things in her life with her *daed*. After all, he probably needed that closeness just as much as she did.

CHAPTER 21

Lizzie took the hand her husband offered as he assisted her into the buggy. Jacob tucked the lap quilt around her, being protective and considerate as always. She looked into his eyes lovingly, thinking he was more handsome than the day she fell in love with him. And to think that they had come full-circle with that love, and were now grandparents.

Jacob squeezed Lizzie's hand. "I still remember the first ride we took in this buggy. I was so nervous."

Lizzie smiled. "I was too. Things were so uncertain then. But now—well, now they are exactly as I imagined they would be in our future."

Jacob tugged on his beard that was peppered with gray. "Do you ever wonder what your life would have been like if you hadn't returned to the community? If we hadn't gotten married?"

"I think about it all the time," Lizzie said cautiously.

"I've never regretted the decision to marry you."

Lizzie nudged Jacob playfully. "I have a couple of regrets."

"You have?" Jacob said nervously as he slapped the reins against his gelding just lightly enough to move him forward. "You don't regret marrying me, do you?"

Lizzie sighed. "*Nee.* I just wish I could take back all the mistakes I've made in my life."

Jacob tucked his arm around his wife. "Those mistakes are what define who you are today. Without the little mistakes we've made, you and I would not be on our way to see our first *grandkinner.*"

Emotion caught up in Lizzie's throat. "I know that, but I would have preferred to have done everything right."

Jacob steered the gelding down the country lane. "If everyone did everything right all the time, then *Gott* wouldn't know our true heart. We have to endure these trials in life to make us stronger and to prepare us for eternity in Heaven."

"You're saying this was all in *Gott's* plan for us?"

Jacob nodded. "*Gott* knew every step we were going to take, every stumble, every fall—just to get to this place in our lives right at this very moment. He orchestrated every aspect of our lives to bring us to this very spot at this very time so that when we got here, it would be to drive over to see that new *boppli.*"

Lizzie adjusted the lap quilt a little more snuggly around her. "Why do you suppose *Gott* doesn't try to stop us from making the mistakes we do?"

"He gives us our own will, and when we walk from the path He has laid out for us, He's always at the end of that path waiting for us to turn from our mistakes and return to Him."

Lizzie looked up into her husband's aging eyes that could still put a song in her heart. "How did you get to be so wise?"

Jacob smirked. "I'm not so wise, I'm just old."

Lizzie clicked her tongue on her teeth. "If you're old, that makes me old. I'm not certain I'm ready to be old just yet."

Smiling, Jacob placed a loving arm around his *fraa.* "I'm a *grossdaddi.*"

"*Jah,* and I'm a *grossmammi.* But I'm happy about it."

Jacob gave Lizzie a quick squeeze. "I am too. I wouldn't have it any other way."

"I hate to think what my life would have been like if I hadn't come back here."

Jacob brushed her cheek with a tender kiss. "The important thing is that you did."

Lizzie looked up into the crisp, blue sky watching her breath form a fog in the cold air. "It seems like just yesterday when I'd first met Caleb. Now he's a grown *mann* with a *fraa* and a new *boppli*. Where has the time gone?"

Jacob let a chuckle escape him. "Do you remember the first thing he said to you?"

Lizzie's eyes filled with happy tears. "He put his little hand in mine and introduced himself to me, and then told me how happy he was that I was going to be his new *mamm.*"

Jacob placed another kiss on Lizzie's cheek. "I'm so glad you put my name on Abby's birth certificate. But I'm even happier I had the opportunity to be her *daed.* I wouldn't have had our lives be any different."

Lizzie wiped her face with her apron. "I wouldn't either. I guess *Gott* knew what he was doing when He told me to put your name on that birth certificate."

Jacob craned his neck to look at his *fraa.* "You never told me that before."

"*Jah,*" Lizzie said. "I prayed about it, and that was the first thing that came to me. It was like a bright light went off in my mind. I couldn't put Eddie's name on there since I was too afraid he'd find us and take her from me. So I prayed asking for guidance. I really believe that *Gott* put your name in my mind at that time. I didn't think twice about it. I just put it on there and never thought about it again until Abby was old enough to start asking about her father."

Jacob chuckled. "She's always been a curious little one."

"I'm certain that little *boppli* she's carrying is going to be just like her—the way it kicks day and night. That's the same way Abby was. Rachel and Samuel didn't kick me that much, and there were two of them! I hope she's prepared to have her hands full with that one."

Jacob turned the horse into the driveway of Caleb's *haus* and parked near the large oak tree. "She will be just fine because she will have you to help her."

Lizzie turned to her husband and looked into his blue-green eyes. "*Danki* for marrying me that day."

Jacob leaned in until his lips met Lizzie's. "*Danki* you married me, too."

Lizzie gazed lovingly upon her husband. He was her past, her present, and her future, and she couldn't be more grateful to *Gott* for orchestrating it that way.

CHAPTER 22

Lila had to remind herself as she readied for Rachel's wedding that she was not just a guest. She was to be a server, and that meant she would be warm and sweaty from the heat in the kitchen. And so, she chose her lightest dress and apron. Though it was quite cold for the first day of November, Lila didn't want to overheat in the kitchen. Samuel would be watching her today, she was certain, and she didn't want to look flustered and washed out. She wanted to look like she was able to handle serving his entire *familye* and the community with ease—she wanted to look like marriage material.

Downstairs, the B&B was already bustling with activity as the *menner* were busy setting up the benches for the wedding. All the furniture had been removed the day before and placed in the barn, making it easier for Lila to scrub the floors. It had taken her hours, but when she finished, it was so clean you could have eaten off the floor. Not that she would do such a thing, but the thought had crossed her mind, amusing her at the end of a very tiring chore.

Straightening her apron, Lila was satisfied she'd picked the right dress. It was already the second time she'd changed her clothes this morning, and she feared it wouldn't be her last before the day was through. Lila hurried down the stairs, worried she'd already been absent from the activities too long. If Rachel should need her for something, she wanted to be certain she would be available to her. To think that Rachel could someday be her *schweschder*-in-law made her somehow want to work even harder at making certain this wedding was perfect.

Katie's *schweschder,* Rose had been the most help to Lila this morning. Together, they had managed to clean and prepare about fifty pounds of celery. The kitchen still lingered with the aroma of it as Lila entered.

"Now that you have a dry dress, maybe we can finish the table arrangements," Rose said to her.

"*Jah,* I think that is the last thing we have to do before the guests begin to arrive."

Half the community was already there, but they were each working on some aspect of the preparations. It had been a long morning, and Lila found herself looking forward to being able to sit through most of the three-hour ceremony.

She'd seen Samuel a few times from a distance, but she was certain he hadn't seen her. He was busy with Rose's husband, Noah, and the other *menner* putting in the benches in the front parlor and large dining area so all the guests would fit. She wished today was *her* wedding day, but Samuel still had not asked her. Would he ever? Today, Lila determined, she would keep her mind on task, and keep her eyes where they belonged—on her work.

৪৩৫৩

Samuel couldn't keep his mind on task. All he could do was search out Lila, hoping to catch little glimpses of her as they each worked to finish the wedding preparations. He wished today could be *his* wedding day. But the fact remained he hadn't dared to ask Lila even once more. Too afraid of being rejected every time he asked, he wasn't certain if he would ever be able to ask her again. Though he was certain she didn't realize it, her rejection had humiliated him.

Perhaps she will let me know when she's ready to be asked. After all, she did declare her love first.

Samuel let his mind fill with the memory of the sweet words that had rolled off Lila's tongue. He'd never heard sweeter words. He wanted more than anything to marry her, but he feared she may never be ready. Of course, he didn't think she'd ever tell him she loved him either, so maybe there was still hope.

Trying to get Lila's attention, Samuel nearly tripped over one of his small cousins. Why wouldn't she look at him? Had she changed her mind? How would he convince her to change it back?

Please, Gott, give me the strength to get through this day, and to be supportive of mei schweschder on her special day. Help me to keep my mind on the needs of mei familye so I don't wander from your path.

ЯОСЯ

Near the conclusion of the ceremony, Lila and a few other women rose from their seats to ready the feast that had been prepared in honor of the wedding couple. Lila knew that Samuel would be busy moving the benches and setting up tables for everyone to eat. A long table had already been placed in the large kitchen, and Lila was busy uncovering dishes of food, and arranged the plates on the counters for easy access to all the guests. Several pitchers of sweet tea were being prepared, and rolls were being warmed in the oven.

Samuel suddenly burst into the kitchen, stopping abruptly when all eyes fell on him. "I need to see you outside for a minute, Lila."

Lila momentarily searched the faces of Samuel's *familye,* looking for approval of Samuel's request, but none came. "Can't this wait?" Lila said through a gritted-toothed smile. "We have to tend to the wedding guests."

Lizzie shooed her son with a linen dishtowel.

"You can talk to her when everyone has been served, Samuel. Now get out of this kitchen."

"But *mamm,*" Samuel pleaded. "I'm not sure I can wait that long."

Lizzie looked at him sternly. "Then you will have to keep those idle hands busy until Lila can talk to you later. Now go back and help the *menner,* and get out of this kitchen."

Samuel walked away feeling embarrassed by the giggles behind his back. He needed to ask Lila to marry him before he lost his nerve.

CHAPTER 23

Lila couldn't think straight. Was Samuel going to end things with her? She loved him, and he'd said the same to her. He'd kissed her like a *mann* in love, but was it enough for him? Was he finally going to end it simply because she had turned down his proposals, or was he prepared to give her another chance and propose again? She prayed it was so.

Lila gazed upon Rachel and Blake, feeling somewhat envious of their commitment to one another. They knew exactly what they wanted, and they'd sealed their future together with marriage. Why couldn't she and Samuel be that happy?

Gott, free me from my stubbornness. Give me the courage to face my fears about marriage and having bopplies. The desire for those things is not enough. I need courage beyond my comprehension, Gott.

Lila worked in silence beside Samuel's *mamm.* Was the woman angry with her? She didn't think Lizzie was the type of woman to anger easily, but somehow, Lila wondered if maybe deep down, she disapproved of the blossoming relationship between Samuel and herself. When all was finished, Lila excused herself and went outside to look for Samuel. She had caught a glimpse of him out on the lawn setting up tables for the youth to have their meal.

As her feet padded across the dock, Lila remembered the sweetness of the kiss she'd shared with Samuel on this very spot. Gazing out across the pond, she had to admit that it was indeed a very romantic spot. Had he only gotten caught up in the moment of their kiss instead of falling in love with her the way he'd claimed? She prayed it wasn't so.

Behind her, she could hear the sound of a *mann's* shoes padding across the dock toward her. She didn't dare turn around for fear it wasn't Samuel.

"I was hoping to find you out here so we could talk."

The familiar smooth baritone of Samuel's voice sent shivers through Lila. As he neared, she sensed his presence like a warm breath on the back of her neck. He leaned in and kissed the top of her head.

Lila whipped her head around. "Don't do that here. Half the community is only a short distance from us. What if someone sees?"

Samuel curled his fingers around hers. "Then they will see a couple of people who are in love."

Lila felt giddiness overtake her, but she braced herself for Samuel's rejection. Though he loved her, would he refuse to move forward with a relationship since during their last conversation she'd informed him she didn't want to marry him? How could she tell him she changed her mind without seeming desperate? She *was* desperate for him to know of her change of heart.

"I know you were eager to talk to me earlier. Are you still as eager to tell me whatever it was you felt couldn't wait? Or have you changed your mind?"

Samuel held tight both her hands in his, pulling them to his mouth to blow his warm breath on them.

"You're fingers are like ice."

"I was hoping it would be a warmer day for your *schweschder's* wedding, but I'm grateful the sun is warm at least."

Samuel gazed into her eyes lovingly. "I wish we were alone so I could collect on my daily kiss."

Lila wasn't certain how much more small talk she could handle. "I want to marry you," she blurted out.

Samuel's eyes narrowed. "I haven't asked you. Why do you keep doing that to me?"

Lila's eyes misted. "I'm sorry. I understand if you don't want to marry me."

Samuel lifted Lila's chin and kissed her lips gently, not caring who would see their intimate moment. "I *do* want to marry you, but I want to be the one to do the asking."

Lila's lower lip quivered. "You said you wouldn't ask me again."

Samuel smiled. "Only because you said not to. But I was prepared to do just that earlier when I wanted to talk to you—when *mei mamm* kicked me out of the kitchen like I was still one of her wee *kinner.*"

Lila's face brightened as Samuel took a knee in front of her. Still holding her hands tightly, he looked up at her, his blue eyes sparkling in the afternoon sun.

"Will you marry me, Lila?"

Lila nodded. "*Jah*, I will. I will marry you and kiss you every day for the rest of our lives."

Samuel stood abruptly and pulled her into his arms, not caring who might witness their embrace.

"When did you change your mind?"

Lila kissed him full on the mouth.

"It was when you kissed me right here in this very spot under the harvest moon."

The End

BONUS RECIPE:

I would like to thank my friend, Diana Montgomery for sharing her recipe with me and my readers. Bless you, Diana.

Diana Montgomery's Story:

Fall brings me to my favorite time of year. I love the fall colors; the smell of the air just has a different scent. It also means Pumpkin Rolls in my family. This tradition started many years ago. I would go to bible studies in the morning at a friend's house (Deb Herrold), my best friend. There would probably be a half dozen of us there to study. Then after the study ended most all the ladies would go home. That was when we would start the fun. First, we'd make a visit to the pumpkin patch. I like to get a real pumpkin instead of using a can of processed pumpkin. Then we carve it up and cook the pumpkin down until it's soft. Then we are ready to start the assembly line of making the pumpkin rolls. A normal batch would be 26 in a day. Plus a couple of pumpkin pies to take home for supper. My family just loves them. When I worked, I would get lots of orders for them. Years later I still get calls for them. I already started for this season.

Dutch Country Pumpkin Rolls

2/3 cup pumpkin (cooked or canned)
3/4 cup flour
1/2 teaspoon cinnamon
3 eggs 1 teaspoon salt
1 cup sugar
1 teaspoon baking soda

Filling

6 ounces cream cheese (softened)
2 Tablespoons butter
1 teaspoon vanilla
1 cup powdered sugar

Bake at 375 for 15 minutes, or until golden brown.
Take standard size cookie sheet, cut wax paper to fit it, and don't let any hang over the pan. Spray the wax paper with non-stick cooking spray. Set this aside.

Mix pumpkin, eggs, and sugar in one bowl. In another bowl mix dry ingredients, flour, salt, baking soda and cinnamon.

Once this is done, mix dry ingredients in with pumpkin mixture. Now take this and pour onto the cookie sheet. Place in oven 15 minutes, or until you see it is golden looking. Baking times may vary.

While this is baking take a cotton dish towel (lint free). I have towels I use only for this. Spread this on counter and sprinkle the towel with powdered sugar. Now once you take the roll part out of the oven flip it on the towel, cake side down. Peel off the wax paper. Roll it up like a roll and let it cool. While this is cooling you make the filling. Take all the ingredients put them in a bowl and use your mixer to mix it until creamy. Now take the roll that is cooled and unroll it. Spread the cream cheese all over it. Roll it back up. Now you have a beautiful yummy dessert. I usually make at least 4 at a time. Wrap them in wax paper and put them in freezer bags, and then put them in the freezer until needed. Take out of freezer; slice and serve.

Diana Montgomery

In the love of friendship.

Proverbs 17:17 "A friend loveth at all times"

Picture taken by Diana Montgomery 9/14/12.
I love the little name card she made for me!

Please enjoy this sneak peek of...
The Quilter's Son (Amish Romance)

Chapter 1

Goshen, Indiana

"Why did you hit me?" Liam worked his jaw back and forth, the sting of the slap causing his ear to ring. But more than that, she'd crushed his spirit with one blow.

Lucy doubled her fists and planted them on her hips. She knew she would later need to take a knee and beg forgiveness, but for now, she was content with her outburst. "Did it knock any sense into you? I can give it another try if it will change your mind."

Furry showed in Lucy's eyes, her face twisted in anger. But there was something else that showed in her eyes. Fear lay just below the surface where she tried very hard to hide it.

Liam felt caught between elation that she cared so much, grief over knowing how much he would miss her when he was gone, and irritation that she would defy the commitment of peace among the Amish.

"I'm not changing my mind. You can hit me a hundred times and it won't make me stay here. I want to be on my own and explore the world. Ever since my *daed* died last month, it's made me wonder if there was more to life than what we see in our secluded little corner of this community. I feel stifled here. Computers and cell phones interest me. And I've always wanted to learn how to build more than barns. I want to design houses, and to do that, I have to learn from outside construction companies. The only opportunity I have here is plowing the same fields my *daed* did his entire life. I want more out of life than that, and my *daed* knew that. When I die, I want my life to mean something."

Lucy looked at him through the veil of tears that blurred her vision. "You really think your *daed's* life amounted to nothing?"

"*Mei daed* knew I didn't want to be a farmer. That's why he let me go to the public school behind my *mamm's* back. With only three weeks left of my senior year after he died, I continued to go so I could graduate because I'm more determined than ever to get out of this backward society."

Lucy's lips formed a grim line, and tears spilled from her eyes. "If you think being Amish is *backward,* then perhaps you're correct in saying you don't belong here. But at least have the decency to face your *mamm* instead of sneaking out the window this late at night."

Liam kicked at the knapsack that rested against the large oak tree that stood beside the *haus*. It was almost too dark to see the expression on Lucy's face, but what he saw of it, he didn't like. "You didn't complain any of those nights I snuck out the window to meet with you."

"That's because I thought you had intended to marry me. Now I find out you stole that first kiss from me that I was saving for my husband; I can never get that back."

Liam braced his hands on her forearms. "Then come with me. We can still get married. We can get a little apartment and live in the city."

Lucy broke from his grasp, her face curling with disgust. "I could never get married without my *familye*. And I won't marry a *mann* who isn't baptized."

Liam picked up his knapsack and flung the weight of it over one shoulder. "Then I suppose we will be parting ways. If I take the baptism I will be destined to be just like my *daed*."

Lucy sobbed. "Would that really be so bad? How do you think he would feel if he could see you now running away from your *familye* like a coward?"

Liam yanked the straw hat from his head and tossed it to the ground. "He isn't here. My *mamm* and *schweschder* will be better off without me. As long as I don't want to be here, my heart isn't in it. So what's the point in staying? So I can make them as miserable as I am? Besides, Lydia no longer talks to me, and *mamm* doesn't talk to either of us. All she does is sit at her quilting frame and sew quilts. Neither of them will even notice I'm gone."

Lucy sniffled, closing the space between them.

"Even if they don't, I will."

Liam backed away from her. If he kissed her now, he would never have the courage to leave. He didn't want things to end between them; he loved her a great deal, but he guessed it wasn't enough to make him want to stay. If he changed his mind it wouldn't be because of the opinion or request of another person. He had to stay for himself, and that wasn't how he felt. His desire to go was too strong to let anything or anyone get in his way—even if that meant he would have to break the heart of the woman he loved.

Lucy found it difficult to breathe. How could Liam do this to his *familye*—to her? Suddenly all the excuses he'd given her over the past few years regarding his busyness had made sense. He was too busy because he'd been leading a double life. Going to school all day and then working his chores around such a demanding schedule. Was he leaving her because he didn't think she was smart enough for him? Did he want someone better than her?

"Will you at least give it some more thought? Have you even prayed about it?"

Liam looked away. He hadn't prayed about it in the past month. He hadn't reached out to *Gott* about much since his *daed* died. He didn't want to hear the answer his heart was nudging him toward. He'd had his mind made up for some time, and now that he was eighteen, it was time.

Lucy nodded. "Your silence tells me you haven't prayed. Since you are so determined to abandon your *familye* and your faith, will you at least tell me where you're going so I can visit you?"

Liam paused. "*Nee,* it will be too far. I'm heading toward Michigan."

He didn't tell her that he was too nervous to go too far. Most likely, he would stay in Indiana and go to South Bend where his friends planned on renting a small house. He feared that if Lucy knew he would be living only a few miles away, she would constantly nag him about returning home.

Lucy lifted her chin in defiance. "If you're determined to go, then don't come back because I won't be waiting for you."

Her statement hurt worse than the slap she'd delivered across his face just a few moments earlier. Liam watched his future walk away from him, as he told himself a better future waited for him in the next town over. They'd both made their decision, and now they would have to live with it. Liam was confident he had his *daed's* blessing to leave, and that was all that mattered at the moment.

Chapter 2

South Bend, Indiana

"I still look Amish," Liam complained as he studied his appearance in the dressing room mirror.

"I'm going to need a haircut."

He had chosen the clothing store in the mall, after his new roommate, Steve, advised him that the store carried the latest styles. He liked the casual look of the sweatshirt and jeans, but his hair still gave him away. A quick stop at the barber shop would get rid of all traces of the Amish in him. But it couldn't erase the pull he still felt in his heart. At eighteen, his biggest desire was to stay as far away from the Amish community as possible, and leave the pain of losing his *daed* behind him once and for all.

His *mamm* had no idea he'd been sneaking away to the public school for the past four years to get his diploma. His *daed* had helped him hide it from his *mamm,* but after the accident, his *mamm* was too consumed with grief to even notice Liam's antics when he continued to go. His twin sister, Lydia, was too busy caring for the house and doing all the things their *mamm* used to do before the buggy accident that took their father's life, so she hadn't noticed either.

It was a tough time for everyone, and Liam was responsible for the upkeep of the farm. Spending all day in school and keeping up with his studies was difficult to do with a farm to maintain, but he'd been determined to leave home and start a new life for himself, leaving Lydia to take over in his absence.

He was now finished with his senior year and needed the diploma to get a job out in the *real world,* as he'd come to know it. His friends at school had guided him every step of the way, right down to teaching him how to drive a car and how to dress and act so he could hide his heritage from the outside world. The transition had not been an easy one, but it was what he felt he needed to do to stifle the grief he still held onto over his father's death.

Liam's refusal of the Bishop's prompting to receive the baptism to seal his Amish roots had not gone over well with anyone. He felt guilty for leaving his *mamm* and *schweschder*, but he didn't see his leaving would change things much. He'd been a coward and left his *mamm* a note letting her know he was leaving, but he didn't think about how it would affect her. His being there had gone unnoticed when his family stopped functioning after his *daed's* accident.

Liam determinedly put the memories behind him, unable to imagine the regret that would hound him over the next few years...

Chapter 3

Seven years later...

A summer breeze rustled the leaves on the trees in front of the shops that lined Main Street in Goshen. Being a typical July morning in Indiana, steamy mist rose from the dew-drenched patches of grass that lined the walkways as the sun warmed up the earth. Liam stood across the street behind a maple tree, hoping his mother and his sister would not notice him watching them. He knew the nature of the Amish was to walk with downcast eyes when in public because he'd spent the first eighteen years of his life doing the same, but he feared his mother would somehow sense his presence and look his way. Since he'd left home, he'd grown into a man—an *Englischer*. But that wouldn't stop a mother from recognizing her own son, would it?

When his mother and sister entered the small quilt shop, he noticed his mother had used a key to open the door. He knew the insurance company of the driver of the car that had killed his father had presented his mother with a sizable settlement, and he wondered now if she'd finally used it to open the shop. Part of him wanted to go to her and ease the worry lines that creased her aging face, but too much time had passed. A reunion would only open old wounds. Since he hadn't taken the baptism, his actions had not earned him a shunning, but that wouldn't keep his family from turning a cold shoulder to him—something he felt he deserved.

Even if he were to approach them, he knew he couldn't handle the pain of rejection from his own mother and sister. Shame crept into his heart for his act of betrayal toward his family and the community. He felt like a coward, and he had to admit that his life away from them had been empty and lonely. He'd thrown himself into his work, earning enough money working for others to start his own business. Now with seven men that counted on him, he felt the strain even more.

They'd only had a few big jobs so far this year, and if he didn't bring in more work soon, his company would perish, along with all his hard work. But what had it all been for? To escape a community shunned by the outside world, only to trade it for being shunned by the people he loved most? Now, as he stood across the street watching his mother and sister enter *The Quilter's Square,*

Liam suddenly questioned the decision he'd made seven long years ago...

ഇവെ

Nellie Yoder felt a breeze brush by her, and with it came the feeling she was being watched. Out of the corner of her eye, she spotted the *Englischer* again; he was standing across the street as if waiting for an invitation from her. She felt his presence, the same as if she were still carrying him in her womb. After all, a mother knows her own flesh and blood. She had managed to swallow the lump that formed in her throat and compose herself for the sake of the *dochder* who had not left her side during the years since her husband's death. Nellie longed to hold her son and tell him how much he'd been missed, but only time would tell if such a dream could become reality.

She ushered Lydia into the quilt shop before the girl noticed her twin brother loitering across the street. What had she been thinking when she'd opened this shop? She knew that it needed repairs that she couldn't fix on her own. She'd known about Liam's business for several months, and thought it would give her the opportunity to bring her son home where he belonged. Her plan was to hire him to do the renovations, hoping it would draw him back to his *familye* and the community.

Now, as she saw him for the third day in a row, Nellie suddenly wondered if she should have thought things through a little more clearly. After all these years of letting her husband's settlement sit idle, she wondered if using it to get her son back was the wisest thing she could have done. She feared that because so much time had passed, he would be more resistant to returning to the community. But after seeing him watching her again this morning, she was convinced she'd made the right move. She knew she would have to proceed with caution, so as not to upset Lydia or spook Liam. She didn't want him to run from her, but so far, he'd not approached her either. She sighed deeply as she watched him walk away, knowing it was too late to abandon her plan now. The first step had already been taken.

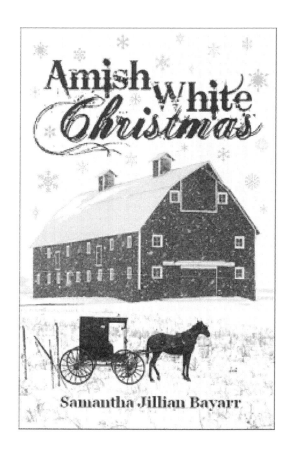

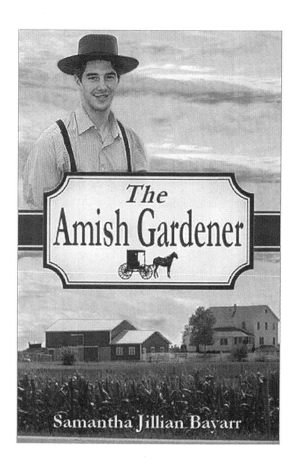